Reckless

Following Jesus to the Point of No Return

Zane Black

A D2S Publishing book
PO Box 745323
Arvada, CO 80006

Editor: Jane Dratz
"Skateboarding" Cover painting by Ron Francis,
www.RonaldFrancis.com

Black, Zane.
Reckless: Following Jesus to the Point of No Return
ISBN: 978-0-9827733-7-6
Library of Congress Control Number: 2012951076

Printed in the United States of America
1 2 3 4 5 6 7 8 9 / 12 11 10 09 08 07 06

Dedication

To all the men who have personally invested
in my life through intentional discipleship and
shown me what it truly means to follow Jesus.

To name a few:

Greg Stier, Derwin Gray, Brad Keirnes,
Phil Peterson, Bryan Bartells, Seth Dombach,
Dan Thomas, Wayne Weismann, Frank Cirone,
Matt Roberts, Doug Horch, Doug Toller,
Steve Bullard, Joshua Morris, and so many more
who have helped shape me into the
man I am today.

My hope is that this book will inspire others
to make the same everlasting investment
through discipleship.

Contents

Acknowledgements

To my wife, thanks for reading my drafts and
helping me to craft the chapters.
You make me better.

Mom and Dad, I wouldn't be where I am, if it
weren't for you. Thanks so much for all
your love and support.

And

To my editor, Jane Dratz, you have been far more
than an "editor." You have labored and toiled over
this book and made me sound way smarter than I
actually am. I could not have done it without you.
You are amazing. THANKS!

1
THE INVITATION

**Jesus invites us to go all in, to follow Him
to the point of no return.**

One sunny afternoon awhile back, I'd just entered
Timberline Lodge, a Torchbearers Center, located
in the beautiful mountains of Coloradical, when I
suddenly realized that I'd left my skateboard out in
the lobby. As I headed back to grab it, I discovered
it'd been taken over by a six year old wild man
named Jo-Jo.

I work at Timberline and Jo-Jo's family lives there
too, so I knew him well. He was one of my favorite
little kids, because he had no fear. To say that he
was hyper would be an understatement. I felt like I
could relate.

Whenever you were around Jo-Jo, you knew
something exciting was going to happen. Like
the time when his mom found him in the laundry
room, not so much helping with the daily chores,
but with his pants down, proceeding to pee into
the dryer socket!

A dryer socket is 220 volts of electricity and
probably could have blown the little dude
through the wall.

His mom freaked out, naturally, as any mother would do when she finds her child urinating in large electrical sockets. But Jo-Jo just looked up with a smile and said, "Look, Mom, SPARKS!"

So Jo-Jo was a wild man, and I loved him for it.

But on this particular late afternoon, Jo-Jo had been drawn like a magnet to my skateboard and he'd flipped it upside down so that the wheels were up in the air. He was sitting in the middle of it, spinning those wheels like crazy. It was almost as if he were trying to rip them off the board, all the while making a noise with his mouth like a wild hyena. Everybody else just walked by thinking, "Oh that wild little Jo-Jo." But for me this looked like a golden opportunity.

I don't know what I was thinking, but I got the wild idea that I wanted to see if Jo-Jo was interested in actually riding the skateboard. So I carefully approached this wild little animal and invited him to experience the board on a whole new level by asking, "Hey Jo-Jo, you want to ride the skateboard?"

Now this stopped Jo-Jo mid hyena cackle. I could tell he was interested, but he also realized that he'd have to stop what he was doing in order for me to show him what I wanted to show him. He thought about it for a while and then ever so slowly got off the board, signaling he was willing to give me a chance.

So I very carefully reached out to grab the board, knowing that I was jeopardizing my fingers in front of this little savage. He growled a little, but let me pass.

I took the skateboard, holding it upside down with the wheels still up and then making some sweet noises myself as if I were some sort of magician, I flipped the board right side up.

Carefully, I took Jo-Jo and put him on the skateboard. This is where it got fun. I felt like we needed a little more room to roll, so I slowly pushed him from the lobby to the cafeteria. I figured this would be perfect for our purpose. You see, it was dinnertime and people were setting the tables and trying to work, but I figured they would serve as perfect obstacles for Jo-Jo and me. I pushed him around the room while he yelled at the top of his lungs, "I'M SKATEBOARDING!!!!!" We were running into tables, chairs, and yes, even the servers trying to do their job. But it was awesome!

[Jo-Jo and I experiencing a skateboard the way it was designed to be used.]

When we were done, Jo-Jo hugged my neck so tightly I thought my head was going to pop off. He had just experienced the skateboard in the way it was meant to be used and his joy was uncontainable.

So what does this Jo-Jo story have to do with Jesus?

What Jo-Jo learned about experiencing a skateboard in the way it was meant to be used is also true about us and our life with Jesus. Here's what I mean.

If you've put your trust in Jesus, you already have your "salvation skateboard." It's yours. It was given to you freely. But maybe you haven't yet learned how to ride it and experience the fullness of its purpose.

Maybe you're like Jo-Jo, sitting on it upside down just spinning the wheels, and Christianity has become boring. When all the time, Jesus has given you this gift of a relationship with Him so you can jump on and discover the thrill of the ride. So you can experience all that your life in Christ was designed to be, bombing every hill of opportunity, opening up new horizons never before imagined.

And let me be really clear here. Your salvation is a free gift. It comes by faith alone in Jesus alone. Free to you, but it isn't cheap, because it cost Jesus everything. This is why you shouldn't be content to stop at the point where you first trusted in Christ and leave it at that.

Because Jesus is calling you, as His follower, to even more. Not in order to *be* saved, but because you *are* saved.

He longs for you to experience the fullness of this gift you've received! He's inviting you to go all in and learn how to actually ride your board. He put it this way in John 10:10, *"...I have come that they may have life, and have it to the full."*

What does this look like?

It's all about learning to follow Him. Because following Jesus is about more than just getting out of hell and getting into heaven (fire insurance). It's about experiencing the fullness of life on earth (the very life of GOD) NOW!

Jo-Jo had to stop what he was doing and try something new in order to experience the fullness of what the board was made for. Maybe you too need to try some new things and give up some old things in order to experience the fullness of what Jesus has for you. Jo-Jo had to trust me in what I wanted to show him, and he did, because he believed it just might be better. And I promise you that Jesus has even greater things in store for you if you are willing to trust Him more fully and go all in.

And that's what this book is about. What it looks like to recklessly abandon all to follow this Jesus guy for all you're worth, with everything you've got.

I invite you to join me and step into this adventure of following Him.

Just like all adventures, it will involve risk and even take sacrifice, but the payoff will be worth it. Because the invite that Jesus gives to truly follow is actually an invitation to an all-satisfying and fulfilling life of endless opportunities.

This epic adventure is available to every man, woman, dude or dudette alive who has trusted in Christ for heaven and wants to go a step further and experience how it was designed to impact their lives on earth. This is not just for pastors, priests, theological teachers, adults or the educated. This fullness that Jesus offers is for everybody, even teenagers!

And it's meant to be experienced today.

2

EMBRACING THE QUEST

Following Jesus is not about tiptoeing into the shallow end of the pool. It's about diving headfirst into the deepest part of the ocean.

So often people get focused on the future, thinking about what's next, missing the fullness of life NOW.

Kind of like when you're 12 years old and you just can't wait till you turn 13. You dream about no longer having to answer to your parents because you are going to be a teenager and you'll get to do whatever you want. You think to yourself, that's when life will be good.

Then you turn 13 and your parents are like, "You're grounded...just because you're a teenager."

So then you start dreaming of the day when you will turn 16 and receive the KEYS to freedom! I mean, just think about it, true freedom, going where you want, whenever you want. That's when life will be good.

Then you turn 16 and your parents are like, "Well, your little sister needs to be picked up from volleyball, your brother needs to go to his friend's and we need you to pick up some stuff from the grocery store." Your keys to freedom end up being the keys to becoming the family taxi driver.

Okay, but you don't worry too much, because the light at the end of the tunnel is near. Graduation is just around the corner. You can almost taste the freedom, true freedom from all responsibility and from your parents, too. I mean, you won't have to answer to anyone! That's when life will be good.

Graduation comes and your parents are like, "Time to be an adult, you need to get a job." So you go get a job...but your boss is a JERK!!! So then you think, I know when life will get good, when I retire. Then you retire and you are like, "I'M GOING TO DIE!"

Too often we are continually looking to the future for when "life will get good," but life is also about making the most of the here and now today.

In fact, I think this is where a lot of "religions" miss it. Many religions put restrictions on people, creating boundaries to live within, so that some day off in some faraway place "life will be good."

That always seemed lame to me. Why ruin my life here, so that maybe someday far off in the future while living in the clouds, things will supposedly be super fun? Why not just have fun now and worry about later, well, later?

You see, I have always been the type of person who wants to experience the fullness of life and adventure in the moment. I want the thrill and excitement of life. I want "the good life" NOW!

Unfortunately, this drive for living on the edge has caused me to make some poor decisions along the way. And in my quest to experience "the good life" now, I followed the ways of the world, rather than the leading of Jesus.

In sixth grade I started smoking, in seventh grade I started drinking and by ninth grade I started doing drugs. I continued in that life of drinking, drugs and drama throughout high school and past graduation. Things got out of control. I ended up drinking myself to the point of a coma and almost lost my life.

The very life I was trying to experience almost slipped from my grip.

Looking back, some people might think I went down this road because I was raised in a broken home and so I was looking for love and acceptance. But my parents, although they did split when I was real young, loved me with their whole heart and went to great lengths to give me the best life possible. My parents are great people and I look up to both of them and love them a ton.

Some might think it's because I got involved with the wrong crowd. Well, it's true that my friends weren't always the best influence, but neither was I. I am not even sure who influenced who first. Like which came first, the chicken or the egg?

I think it's because I was on a quest to experience the fullness of life, here and NOW. I think that is still the case.

But back to my story. After high school, I decided to just live life the way I wanted, abandoning any

[Taking risks early on!!]

notion of responsibility and partying my days away. Naturally, this didn't last forever, nor did it satisfy my longings.

I had heard it said, "If you do what you've always done, you'll get what you've always got." To experience something new, you gotta try something different. I thought that sounded great, but how? I had no clue where to go or what to do.

Someone told me I should go back to school and get an education, because that's what normal people do.

So I went for it.

A couple classes a week couldn't be too bad. And with my job of working as a beer delivery guy, there was still lots of fun to be had (because of my fringe benefits—free beer).

One of the classes offered was a religion class. I was skeptical, but also a little intrigued. So I thought I would give it a shot.

I really liked learning about Buddhism, Judaism, Spiritualism and all sorts of other isms. But it also stirred up more questions. I had previously passed off all the "religions" as really just saying the same thing. You know, kinda like everybody trying to get to the same mountaintop, claiming that their way up was the best, but regardless, they'd all end up in the same place.

But the more studying I did for class, the more I realized that all of these religions were very different. And if we were to say that they were all the same, then we would be doing a disservice to all of them, because at the core of each religion is the claim that they are the truth. But I realized that they can't all be right, because they contradict each other.

Still, there was something that stuck out to me about Christianity as being totally different and it kept me interested.

Within Christianity there seemed to be this awe and reverence toward God, as though He is the most important and powerful Being in the world. And while many other religions have that same type of all powerful God figure, Christianity's "holy" God was also very relational, even calling people His friends (John 15). So rather than giving a list of rules and regulations, the God of Christianity invited people to "follow" Him (Mark 1:16-20). To follow a person, a real living being. Not to follow a book or a tradition, but a person.

This invitation intrigued me. It sounded risky. But according to Jesus, it would also be the most rewarding experience in life. And Jesus talked about it not just as something for the distant future, but for the NOW, as well.

Over and over, Jesus talked about how following Him would bring fullness of joy. How it would open the door to experiencing the only life that brings satisfaction.

So when I was 21 years old, I decided to take the plunge and trust in this Jesus guy. And not just for my security in heaven. I wanted more. I wanted to go all in. **Because I realized that truly following Him was the real answer to my quest to experience life to the fullest.**

None of this sticking my toe in and wading around in the shallow end of the pool. I was not *just* interested in the Christianity that's about someday going to heaven. Though don't get me wrong, that's a GREAT thing. But Jesus' invite is to more than heaven and I wanted the full deal.

I cannot say that it has always been easy, but I can say with confidence that it has always been fulfilling. In truly trying to follow Jesus, I've found the joy, happiness and fullness of life that I was looking for. I haven't always followed perfectly. I am not even sure if I know how to do it very well, but I keep looking to Jesus, learning all along the way what it is to recklessly abandon all and follow Him.

That's why I invite you to not only enter into this amazing relationship with God, but to take it to the next level and join me in this quest of learning what it is to truly follow Him.

Crazy as it may sound to you, I actually believe that how you respond to this invite from Jesus to truly go all in will forever effect your enjoyment of this life. **Because the greatest treasures in all of life are waiting to be found in the epic adventure of following Him.**

So let's turn our compasses towards Jesus as we set sail on this epic journey and begin to learn what it means to go all in and follow Him to the point of no return.

I cannot promise that this journey will be safe. I can't promise that things will always go your way. There will be twists, turns and unexpected hardships along the journey. The storms of life will still rage, the rains will still come and waves will continue to crash. It will involve taking risks and even facing your fears. But there will always be hope of safe harbors on the horizon. And based on what I have experienced, I predict that your greatest joys in all of life will be experienced along the way.

[Sailing off on an epic adventure!]

And the launching point for this adventure of endless possibilities is found in Jesus' simple invite—

"'Come, follow me,'..." (Matthew 4:19).

3
FOLLOWING THE LEADER

RECKLESS

Following Jesus is actually the most radical, reckless and standout way to live.

Let's be honest. When we think of "following," our first impressions are often negative. You know, like when someone is just a "follower." They just go along with the crowd, not really having a mind of their own and doing what everyone else does.

Some of us have actually put great effort into not being a follower.

Like, I would rather be different, even at the risk of being weird, as long as I don't have to be a "follower." Right?

But when you think about it, there are some types of following that aren't that bad, you know, like following your favorite band on Facebook or Twitter. That kind of following is alright, because it allows you to stay up with them when they release a new album or when they are playing shows, so you don't miss them if they come to your area.

Sure, some people take that type of following a little too seriously. Like, there are some who are glued to their social networks to the point of becoming antisocial to the world right in front of them. I heard that some tweeters log an average of 100 tweets per day, which is about a tweet every nine minutes for 16 hours straight every day.

Or how about the Facebook creepers? You know, those people who are always creeping on other people's profiles, trying to catch up on the latest gossip, seeing who's dating who. But don't think they are the only ones who are a little weird, because you know you too have done a little FB creeping yourself. Who hasn't?

Another type of following that is interesting is the type that happens in the movies. You know the scene where someone is following someone else, but trying to remain unnoticed? If they're in a car, then they try to remain at a distance where they are close enough to keep up, but not so close that they'll get noticed and blow their cover.

Sadly, I think this "undercover" approach is probably the truest picture of how many Christians today "follow" Jesus. Sure, they have made the decision to trust Him for their salvation, but they have chosen to stay at a "safe" distance, trying not to be noticed by others as an actual follower of Jesus.

But Jesus calls us to follow so closely that everyone will recognize us as His followers. That we will be so identified with Christ that we can't help but be noticed as His disciples.

This type of following takes boldness. It takes a willingness to live dangerously and to make sacrifices because it involves a cost.

I'm just going to put it out there—sometimes it's just not cool to be a Christian. And if we choose to radically follow Jesus, then our social status is on the line, because following Christ means that we will be different from the crowd. It might even mean that we could be rejected by those closest to us.

So why would anyone take the risk of choosing to follow Jesus? Because I believe that deep down, beneath the surface need of wanting to be accepted, there is something far greater that we desire. To be ourselves. **We all long for the freedom to be exactly who we were made to be—to be unique.**

Yet for so many of us, we still fear that our differences will cause us to not fit in. And sometimes the quest to fit in will lead to being just like the crowd. This can take us down some destructive paths. That's what happened to me.

I tried to fit in by skipping classes, smoking cigarettes, drinking underage, doing drugs and swearing like a sailor. This is the stuff that defined me. I ended up just conforming to the pressures around me. I was just another person following the crowd, trying to find my place in it. I was a follower, but the wrong kind.

But then, through a crazy series of events that I touched on earlier and that I more fully recount in my book, *InZane*, God brought me to a point where I ended up accepting the invitation from Jesus to follow Him.

[Lookin' for the good life.]

It was an invitation to be a different kind of follower, a truly radical one. And in the newness of becoming a Christian, it dawned on me that if I wanted to be like Jesus, it meant being different than the world. It meant leaving some of the things of the past behind and living for a new purpose. Following Jesus meant I could no longer follow the world.

Sometimes being different is scary.

But it was in this process that I began to discover that I am different. OK, maybe I'm even weird. And I'm okay with that, because God made me to be different. Rather than being ashamed of my differences, I began to embrace the fact that I'm unique. **I realized that I didn't have to let the approval of others define me. It is God's thoughts about us, and His thoughts alone, that should define us.**

In Psalm 139:13-14 the writer says to God, *"For you created my inmost being; you knit me together in my mother's womb. I praise you because I am fearfully and wonderfully made; your works are wonderful."*

In Jeremiah 1:5 God puts it this way, *"Before I formed you in the womb I knew and approved of you as My chosen instrument, and before you*

were born I separated and set you apart" (AMP).
You are unique in God's eyes and He has specific
and special plans for you. You do not need to
look for approval from anyone else, because
God has already approved of you. You are His
creation, He made you, He formed you and He
does not make mistakes.

How would our lives look different if we truly
believed this? We would follow Jesus and not
the crowd.

From time to time I still struggle with seeking the
approval and acceptance of others. I feel insecure
and worry about what people think of me. And it
steals my joy.

You may think, "But Zane, you speak to thousands
of teenagers all around the nation, you have been
on two reality series, you have thousands of
Facebook friends and fans and have written books
☺!" The truth is, from a human perspective, it's
still not enough to satisfy my need for acceptance
and approval.

You see, when our source of confidence comes
from others approval and acceptance we will
always be left disappointed, because people will
let us down and their love will never truly satisfy.

[With the cast of the *GOSPEL Journey Adventure* reality series.]

The pursuit of pleasing people is like chasing after the wind and trying to capture it to save it for later. We will always end up empty-handed.

But when we abandon all that and focus our lives on pursuing God, it's like going for a glass of water on a hot summer day and instead of finding a glass, we find an endless freshwater mountain spring that will satisfy our thirst and the deepest longings of our soul.

In John 4:14 Jesus makes it clear, *"Whoever drinks the water I give him will never thirst. Indeed, the water I give him will become in him a spring of water welling up to eternal life."*

Even though I don't always drink from that all-satisfying spring of water that Christ offers, just the smallest sips have allowed me to find the confidence and strength I need to resist the temptation to just go with the crowd.

My life looks different now as I seek to be defined as a person who looks like Jesus—or you could say—follows Jesus. Because after all, that's what following Jesus really means—becoming like Christ. Following Him even means being different from other Christians. Jesus did not come to make cookie-cutter church goers.

I've learned that if we follow the crowd we are likely to get lost in it, but if we choose to follow Jesus, we will be set apart as a radical. And the world and the Church are in need of radical people who will step up and change things for the better. Because the best leaders are followers of Jesus.

In fact, the true trendsetters and change agents are those who are willing to step out on a limb and try something new. Jesus' followers stand against the tide, they reject the pressure of the crowd and resist the call to conform.

Rather than get lost in the crowd, they become a beacon of hope, lighting the way for the lost, no matter the cost.

That's why following Jesus is actually the most radical, reckless and standout way to live!

Many people sit on the sidelines because of the fear of being different. But the people who change the world are the ones willing to take a risk.

So here's the question. Are you ready to be different and resist the crowd?

4

WHY FOLLOW *JESUS?*

It turns out Jesus was no random dude.

If you're going to follow someone, it's important to know whether they are **worth** following, right? After all, you don't want to just follow some random dude.

So how does someone figure this out when it comes to Jesus? Well, let's drill down and take a closer look at who He really is. Hopefully, this will help you realize that you can follow Him in total confidence.

In Matthew 4:18-19, we start to get the picture of what this was like for Jesus' very first followers. Here's how it happened:

> *As Jesus was walking beside the Sea of Galilee, he saw two brothers, Simon called Peter and his brother Andrew. They were casting a net into the lake, for they were fishermen. "Come, follow me," Jesus said…*

If some random dude came walking up to me while I was working and invited me to "follow him," I'm pretty sure that I would think he had probably escaped from the loony bin. Unless the dude pulled up in a limo or some other really flashy car and told me that I too could be rich like him. But then I guess I would probably just think he was some weirdo and I would be even more sketched out.

Why would Peter and Andrew be willing to leave what seem to be decent paying jobs to follow this random dude? What was it about Jesus that intrigued these brothers to go for it?

It doesn't seem that Jesus was rich and offering some sort of exotic lifestyle. Because later on in the story Jesus invites another person to follow and adds that, *"Foxes have dens and birds have nests, but the Son of Man has no place to lay his head."* (Matthew 8:20). Meaning... Jesus was homeless and inviting this person to homelessness.

So why follow Him?

Well, it turns out Jesus was no random dude.

Jesus was "The One" God's people, the Jews, were waiting for—they called Him the "Messiah"—the Promised One. For God's people, the coming of the Promised One was to be a revolutionary event with a multitude of ripple effects.

The "Promised One" may not mean much to us, but back then this "One" was the hope of all the Jews. You see, they were oppressed and abused by the powerful Roman forces who were occupying their home country at the time. Their lives were miserable, so they'd been praying for years that God would send a rescuer.

It's sort of like if there was some tough guy bully at your school who beat kids up, stole their lunches and gave daily swirlies (and didn't even flush first). Yeah, bad news. And worse, imagine that the principal was on the side of the bully, supplying him with duct tape to wrap kids up with and making wedgie day mandatory! If you were in that kind of situation, wouldn't you be desperately praying to God to send somebody who could step up and make things right by inflicting some major pain on this bully (and the principal too).

Well, for God's people back in those days, Jesus was starting to look like He might be the way out of their messy situation. Which would make Him kind of a big deal. The anti-wedgie/anti-swirly enforcer.

So this Jesus guy was not just some random dude who was giving an invitation to follow. This was someone to rally behind and have hope in.

You could even say He was *worth* following.

At this point, I don't think Peter and Andrew yet realized that Jesus was God Himself. It seems like maybe they just had a hunch that He might be "The One" who the people of God were waiting for and that He would lead them someplace that would be radical and exciting.

So even though they didn't know all the truths about Jesus that we know now, they followed.

[Enjoying God's Rocky Mountains with a buddy.]

Because the fact that Jesus was claiming to be "The One," was enough to convince these guys that He was worth it.

But now fast forward to today. And this is where we come to the crux of the choice all of us face when it comes to deciding whether Jesus is worth following: Was He who He said He was?

We have the privilege of being able to look back at so much of what Jesus said and did. So let's summarize some of what we now know on this side of the cross. Because when we do, the evidence for Him being the Messiah is astonishing.

Here are just a few things the Bible tells us about who Jesus is:

- The Creator from the beginning, through whom all things were made (John 1:1-3)
- The bread of life (John 6:35) who satisfies the longings of the human soul (Matthew 5:6)
- The light of the world (John 8:12) who enables people to see clearly so they don't stumble in the midst of dark times (1 John 2:8-10)
- The good shepherd (John 10:11) who will care for the needs of those who are His

sheep, protecting and providing for them (Psalm 23)

- The Son of God (John 10:36) who is the *"radiance of God's glory and the exact representation of His being"* (Hebrews 1:3)
- The way, the truth, the life (John 14:6) which means that no one can go to the Father except through Jesus. He not only testified to be the way to God but is God Himself who took on flesh to live in human likeness (John 5:18, Philippians 2:7)
- The fullness of everything that God is (Colossians 1:19)
- The glory of the Father and The One before whom every being will bow and confess that He truly is Lord (Philippians 2:10-11), some willingly in worship with awe and reverence as His followers, and some out of fear, trembling in anticipation of punishment deserved (Revelations 20:11-15).

Jesus proved He was who claimed to be through His miracles, the power He displayed while here on earth in human form, and through His resurrection from the dead. He proved He was The One who had the power and authority to:

- Heal the sick (Mark 1:29-34)
- Forgive sins (Mark 2:5-7)
- Command authority over creation so that even the wind obeyed his voice (Matthew 8:26)
- Raise the dead (John 11:1-43)
- Give eternal life to others (John 5:21)
- Be the ultimate judge (John 5:22)
- Possess all the authority and power in all of heaven and earth (Matthew 28:18-20).

One of the things that establishes the validity of Jesus claiming to be God is the fact that He fulfilled hundreds of prophecies—predictions that were written down by God's prophets many centuries before Jesus was born. It is said that there are over 300 prophecies about Jesus in the Old Testament, (things like where and when he would be born, how he would die, and on and on). He fulfilled every single one of these prophesies!

This was no accident.

The odds of one person fulfilling just eight of these prophesies is the same likelihood as if you were to fill all of Texas (which is big) with silver dollars until the entire state was two feet deep in coins. Then say you put a mark on one of those coins before sending a blindfolded person out to wander around Texas, giving them just one chance to reach down and pick out the right coin. The odds of them picking up the marked coin are really, really slim, right? Those are the same as the odds of someone fulfilling just eight of the 300 prophecies.[1] And Jesus fulfilled all of them!

It's clear that this Jesus guy was no ordinary dude. He's "kind of a big deal." Think about it, the dates of our history are separated around His life (B.C. and A.D.), there are a few billion people around the world that pray to Him and worship Him, and the book that is written about Him—the Bible—is the bestselling book of all time.

He could not have just been a good person, who taught good things, because He claimed to be God. He was not a person who we just look at as some historical character, because He claimed to be the only way to salvation. Jesus does not give us the option of passing Him by as just another leader or teacher; His life and words demand a response.

C.S. Lewis said that Jesus was either liar, lunatic, or Lord. Jesus was either a liar and all the stuff He claimed to be and do was a lie. Or He was a lunatic, because He actually thought He was God and could forgive sins and offer eternal life to people.

Or Jesus was and is Lord. He was who He said He was. Which then leaves us with a call to respond.

If you've never trusted in Christ, check out the box below to learn how to receive Jesus' free gift of eternal life.

How to Receive Jesus' Free Gift of Eternal Life

We've all been made for a purpose. And that purpose is to know God.

I don't even know you, but I know that your life's purpose is to be in a relationship with God, and you will never be fully satisfied until you're living in the purpose that you were designed for.

You were made to be in a deep, rich, life-transforming relationship with God.

The problem is that all of us have done things we were not supposed to do. We have lied or cheated or done even worse. And because of our poor decisions (aka sin), we've been separated from that relationship with a holy and perfect God (Romans 3:23).

There is nothing we can do in and of ourselves to get back to God, we can't ever be good enough to right our wrongs. But God loves us so much that He made a way back through the most epic display of love in the history of the world. God sent His one and only Son Jesus to come pay the penalty for the wrongs we have done (Ephesians 2:8).

That is why Jesus, although having lived a perfect life, died on a cross 2,000 years ago. Jesus, who the Bible tells us was both fully God and fully human, gave His life for you and for me. If you confess your wrongs to Him and trust Him to save you from the penalty of your sins, you will receive the gift of eternal life. You'll be saved from hell and saved to heaven (Romans 10:9). And you'll also experience the purpose for which you were made today (John 17:3).

This decision to trust in Jesus opens the door to fullness of life on earth, the fullness that so many look for in all the wrong places and come up empty-handed (John 10:10). Jesus promises that the fullness of joy (John 15:11) can be yours, because He offers the fullness of Himself to you. Not only that, but you will no longer have to go through life alone, because He will live in you, helping you all along the way (Matthew 28:20).

If you have never done that before, you can choose to believe right now wherever you're at. You can choose a way that is far better, the way of Jesus that opens the door to the greatest adventure in all of life—following Him.

I once heard it said, "If there is no God, then nothing matters, but if there is a God then nothing else matters."

All of us have to make a decision about whether we really, truly believe that Jesus is who He says He is and that He is worth following. So how about you? Are you absolutely confident that Jesus is **worth** following?

Either turn away from Him and follow your own dreams and desires, living life on your own as you see fit, which will always end in disappointment. Or decide to go all in and follow Him, recklessly abandoning your life, dreams and goals, and trust Him with everything, experiencing the fullness of life you were made for.

But you need to know that truly following Jesus will involve recklessly abandoning your old life in order to have more of Him. Jesus explained it this way in Matthew 13:44, *"The kingdom of heaven is like a treasure hidden in a field. When a man found it, he hid it again, and then in his JOY went and sold all he had and bought that field."*

When we see Jesus for who He really is, we will realize that He's the greatest treasure of all. What a joy to give whatever it takes to experience more of Him.

So read on.

5

RECKLESS ABANDONMENT

RECKLESS

Taking it to the point of no return.

The last couple years I've started to get into longboarding. There is something about bombing hills on a skateboard that just gets me fired up. There's thrill in the adrenaline pumping through my system, wind rushing against my face, the sound of the wheels raging against the pavement and the feeling of pushing the limits of what you thought was possible. Oh yeah, and then comes the thought, "If I wreck, it's gonna be bad, real bad. I'm thinking road rash for days."

My buddy who got me into longboarding was this crazy Canadian kid. He had been bombing hills for years and could ride slopes so steep that I once peed my pants just standing at the top watching him.

When you bomb a hill, you get to what he would call the "point of no return." This is where your speed on the longboard goes beyond the speed at which you can run. You see, there are no brakes on a longboard. I mean, unless you are crazy good and can power slide at high speeds—which is ridiculous and not an option for most.

Because there are no brakes, your only hope of slowing down is to jump off. When you jump off, you better hope you can match the speed of the street with the speed of your feet. If not, then you FACE PLANT and I'm not sure if you noticed, but concrete is not very forgiving. Face planting at high speeds basically means that you are going to be sliding on your FACE across the pavement, while your feet surpass your body (if you're lucky enough, kicking yourself in the back of the head, which is always a nice addition), causing you to form a "U" shape, also known as the "scorpion." This is not pretty.

Which is why if you are going too fast to run it out, then you are past the point of no return.

Even at slower speeds "running it out" is sketchy. So, as you can imagine, the steeper hill, the sketchier the "running it out" option is and the quicker the point of no return comes. Which means you have to fully commit before you even step on the board.

When standing at the top of the hill weighing the possibility of whether you can even make it, so many thoughts run through your head. The what if's and the how to's swirl through your nervous brain which is already having a hard time focusing, and then at a certain point you have to make the decision. *Am I going to go for it?* Because once you start, there's no going back. It's all or nothing.

This has become my favorite part about longboarding—the unknown, the anticipation and the commitment.

This is what I call "reckless abandonment."

Longboarding requires this and so does following Jesus. In fact, this is exactly what Jesus is calling His disciples to when He said, *"Come follow me...and I will make you fishers of men."* It's a call to commit. And we see their response in Matthew 4:20. *"At once they left their nets and followed Him."*

Reckless abandonment is where after assessing the danger, thinking through the cost, surveying what might happen, you commit, never looking back. It's where you recklessly abandon all other things for the pursuit of knowing Jesus and following Him, seeking to make Him known by helping others follow, too.

The reason why I call it "reckless abandonment" is because sometimes other options may seem more practical, easier and safer. Jesus doesn't promise that following Him will be easy or make you popular. Nor does He promise that your life will be successful by the world's standards.

He actually promises the opposite in John 15:19, *"If you belonged to the world, it would love you as its own. As it is, you do not belong to the world, but I have chosen you out of the world. That is why the world hates you."*

And in Luke 14, Jesus says that you should count the cost of following Him, summing it up in Luke 14:33 by saying, *"...any of you who does not give up everything he has cannot be my disciple."*

If you truly want to follow Jesus, it means taking stock of everything you own, thinking through all your dreams and desires, evaluating all your friendships and then offering them all up to Him. Saying to God that these things are no longer yours, but His.

It is reckless, because it may not make logical sense. Maybe in your mind, your possessions and hobbies are your very life and you find your value in them. But Jesus wants to be the source of your value, because He is the author of life. And the things you "own" are actually not yours; they are blessings from God on loan to you to be used for accomplishing God's will on earth.

RECKLESS

Reckless abandonment will require you to have a new focus on what is most important, totally restructuring your life and rebuilding your passions with Jesus as the foundation. Following Him takes the same type of reckless mindset as a skater getting ready to bomb a hill.

Check out what Jesus says to another guy who was thinking about following Him in Luke 9:61-62:

> Still another said, "I will follow you, Lord, but first let me go back and say goodbye to my family." Jesus replied, "No one who puts his hand to the plow and looks back is fit for service in the kingdom of God."

It's like Jesus is saying this is the point of no return. If you embark on this journey, then God becomes #1 in your life and everything else is left behind in comparison to Him.

Jesus is testing this guy to see what he values most. To see if the pursuit of God and the accomplishing of His will is truly his treasure above all else.

The same is true for you. Following Jesus involves your everything. He is calling you to take the focus off life being about you and refocus it on being

100% about Him. So that every decision you make from here on out is for God and not for self.

If you're not willing to recklessly abandon all, then you will have a hard time following Him. It's difficult to live for His purpose if you're still trying to live your life for you. Not that you ever become perfect in your following, because learning to follow is a growing process. We certainly see in the Bible that Jesus' own 12 disciples were far from perfect and they too struggled with going all in.

Maybe at some point in your past you encountered Jesus in one way, shape or form and you put your faith and trust in Him. But maybe the fire has died out and your faith has grown cold.

This is the story of so many Christians. They became believers and were excited at one time, but they have gone back to their old ways.

I am not saying that you need to get saved again or become a Christian all over again. Being saved happens when you first place your trust in Jesus. Becoming a Christian actually has nothing to do with you and your effort, but everything to do with Jesus and His accomplishments (dying on the cross for our sins and rising again). When you believe in Jesus, trusting in Him with your life, you are saved. Done deal. Your debt has been paid, past, present and future sins have been paid in full by His blood. That is something that God does and it happens one time for all time.

But from the point of your salvation on, you have the opportunity to live a new way—a Jesus-focused way. This is the call to "reckless abandonment." This is not only choosing to say no to sin, but also saying yes to surrendering your entire life. The only way you can do that is through the strength of God's Spirit living in you.

Making this change is going to be difficult. It may even seem like this could ruin your life. And in some ways it will, but in the best ways. Your selfish ways will get ruined, your previous priorities will get ruined and your sinful desires will get ruined.

You see, God doesn't ruin lives; He rebuilds them with Himself as the foundation. And God builds masterpieces. When He is the architect, He masterfully weaves together a beautiful creation that causes the world to stand in awe and wonder. He defies the ordinary with the extraordinary. It's just that sometimes He has to tear down the old, in order to build out the new. And sometimes this is painful, because He is ripping out the self-centered ways so He can rebuild God-centered ways.

But you will never be fully satisfied and fulfilled until your life is brought back into the purpose for which it was made. Your life was made for a deep, intimate, eternal relationship with God.

Are you ready to step on board, fully committing everything to Him, in the quest to follow Jesus and tell others about Him? It will feel like getting ready to bomb the hill of your life. You have done all the thinking there is to do and now it's time to commit.

My Canadian buddy who taught me to bomb hills with "reckless abandonment" knew all about fully

[My Canadian buddy bombed hills wearing nothing but his boxers!]

committing. He said that the way he learned how to commit was by bombing hills in his underwear. Yup, you heard me right, just his underwear, no shoes, no shirt, no way out. Crazy Canadian. He said the reason he took this crazy apparel approach was because it forced him to fully commit and that is how he got so good. You see, when you bomb a hill in nothing but your boxers, then you know from the start that there is no going back, there is no way out and no chance of slowing down. It's all or nothing. So he learned that fully committing was the only way to keep his skin.

As a result, he became the best longboarder I know. He is fearless, because he was willing to risk it all and he experienced the pay off.

It's the same with going all in with Jesus. And as you begin to bomb hills with reckless abandonment for Him, don't do it because I said so, or because you feel like it is what you're "supposed to do," or to earn "points" with God. God will never love you any more or any less than He does right now. He loves you despite what you can or can't give back to Him. In fact, the Bible says in Romans 5:8, *"But God demonstrates his own love for us in this: While we were still sinners, Christ died for us."* You're not following Him to **earn** His love. Do it **because of** His love.

Pumped Up about Jesus' Love

Here are some verses that get me really pumped up when I think about Jesus' love for us and the amazing things He promises when we love Him in return and choose to follow Him! Check these verses out:

- *"I have told you this so that my joy may be in you and your joy may be complete"* (John 15:11). Following Jesus is about joy!

- *"I have come that they* [you] *may have life and have it to the full"* (John 10:10). He truly can deliver amazing, abundant life!

- *"Blessed are those who hunger and thirst for righteousness"* (Matthew 5:6). It's when we crave a deep, personal relationship with Him that we are blessed!

- *"You will fill me with joy in your presence"* (Psalm 16:11 and Acts 2:28). Jesus is the fulfillment of the promise and the source of our joy!

So allow yourself to be blown away by Him and His love for you—thinking often about how crazy His love for you is. Allow it to wash over you like the incoming tide, totally covering you in the depths of its goodness. As you bask in its fullness, you will understand why He is worthy of following to the point of no return.

He went all in for you, so you want to go all in for Him! He held nothing back in His love for you, so hold nothing back in your love for Him.

God's love for you is reckless. Is your love for Him reckless?

Are you all in?

6
WHAT NOW?

The Christian life isn't difficult, it's impossible.

If you want to be a follower of Jesus, then you have to follow *Jesus*.

One of my favorite holidays growing up was Halloween. I mean as a kid, who doesn't love dressing up, freaking out your neighbors, playing a couple practical jokes and getting free candy out of the deal?

I was always the kid who would save my candy. My sister on the other hand would eat all of hers in the first week. That was good for me, because then I could bribe her to clean my room and do my chores with my leftover candy.

I still like Halloween. Not because of going door to door to get candy, I tried that a couple years ago and people freaked out, not 'cause I scared them, but because they thought I was too old. Apparently they are the ones who are "too old," because they've forgotten how to have fun. I like Halloween because I love dressing up.

I had these friends who would have parties all the time. Instead of throwing the typical "party" with drugs and alcohol, they would get creative. They would have different theme nights where everybody would dress according to the theme. For instance, there would be 80's night, disco night, sports night, famous person night, or even pajama party night which someone would always take too far, showing up in their boxers.

The best were the people who would not only dress up, but who would act the part the whole night! One of the funniest was "talk show host night" and someone dressed up as Dr. Phil. (For those of you who don't know, Dr. Phil is a talk show psychologist who gives advice on everything from weight loss to divorce to rebellious teenagers.)

Not only did this guy at the party represent with the sweater vest, he shaved the top part of his head and grew out a legit mustache. The whole night, this guy would not have regular conversation, but would always be diagnosing people's lives, getting them to tell him their problems. It was hilarious, because not only did he look like Dr. Phil, he sounded and acted like Dr. Phil. It was awesome.

Clearly this guy had spent a lot of time studying the ways of Dr. Phil.

It's sort of the same way if you want to "follow" Jesus and be like Him. You are going to need to spend some time learning about and getting to know Him, in order that your life may be a good representation of His life.

Often at this point, people want to just be given some sort of a checklist so they might know what things to do in order to be a Jesus follower. Or some may even have some sort of picture in their mind of what a Christian looks like. Unfortunately, the checklists and the picture of Ned Flanders (*The Simpsons'* Christian neighbor) all fall short. Because following Jesus is much more than obeying a checklist of do's and don'ts. And surely becoming like Jesus does not mean we all try to look like Ned Flanders—although he sports a legit mustache as well.

But while there is not a checklist or a mold that you can fit into when making yourself "like Christ," there are some insights and strategies that will help begin this process of being formed into the likeness of Christ.

This may seem difficult because you don't have Jesus in flesh and blood in front of you like the disciples did. I mean, how can you "follow" someone you don't see? It seems like the disciples had an easier time of following, seeing as how they actually got to hang out with Him in His physical form. It's kind of hard to play follow the leader, if the leader is invisible.

Thankfully, you are not just following an invisible leader, nor are you just mimicking what you read about in the life that Jesus lived 2,000 years ago. You are not left alone in your own pursuit of becoming like Jesus. God has given you His

[Speaking at a Dare 2 Share Conference, helping teenagers understand the importance of spending time in God's Word.]

own Spirit to live in you, to help you live this life you're called to.

Jesus described this in John 14:16-18 when He explained to His followers that after He went away, He would give us a Helper who would never leave us, but would actually live inside us. The very Spirit of God is given to every believer to equip us with the ability and resources we need to walk as Jesus walked. This is a truth that so many Christians know about, but don't make the most of.

Every Christian gets it that Jesus paid their debt in dying on the cross, getting them out of hell and into heaven. This is awesomely true! But it is only part of the picture. Jesus also rose to new life and offers you the power to live a new life through His Spirit. Romans 5:10 says, *"If when we were God's enemies, we were reconciled to him through the death of his Son, how much more, having been reconciled, shall we be saved through his life."* His death brings you back into a relationship with God, but it is His life that enables you to live in a way that is pleasing to God on a daily basis.

The One you follow is The One who gives you the strength to follow. 1 Thessalonians 5:24

says, *"The one who calls you is faithful and he will do it."*

Many Christians, in their quest to follow Jesus and be like Him, try to do it in their own strength. This will always produce frustration and discouragement and will always fall short of what God could do.

Because you cannot live the life Jesus calls you to on your own. It's impossible. That is, if you are trying to live it by your own strength and power.

It's like this. Let's say that for your sixteenth birthday your parents buy you a Bugatti Veyron Super Sport, which just in case you were wondering, is one of the fastest production-level cars. It comes stocked with 1,200 horsepower, with a top speed of 267 mph. It goes 0-60 in 2.4 seconds and the base price is $2,400,000. Yep, that's right, sweet sixteen and you just got a two million dollar car. Boo-yeah!

It's probably not the most powerful car engine in the world, but it will most likely be the most powerful car at your school, considering most of your friends are either riding the school bus or driving the parents' minivan, or as they call it, the Swagger Wagon. But what if rather than driving your new rocket ship disguised as a car, you decided to push it to school. Imagine how tired and frustrated you would become pushing this hot rod all the way to school. What about if you came to a hill or even a bump in the road? I don't care how much P90X you have been doing, you are done for. And just think about how foolish you would look. Okay, true, you still have a two million dollar car while your friends are stuck riding the yellow limo or driving in the soccer mom mobile.

What a shame. And living out of Christ's life by faith, is much like turning the ignition and firing up the super charged engine, thereby accessing the fullness of all its resources—all of God fully available to you.

When you became a Christian, God, so to speak, traded in your old beater car for a new Super Sport hot rod. If you have accepted the great gift of this new car (eternal life), but have yet to experience the fullness that is rightfully yours as a Christian (Christ's life), then you will only grow weary and frustrated with this gift. Unless, by faith, you get into your new ride, turn the ignition and unleash the fullness of the potential of the engine under the hood. This is Christ in you which Paul says is our hope of glory (Colossians 1:27). It is

[Enjoy the ride!]

then and only then, that you are ready for the hills of life, ready to travel the distance and experience the fullness of the roadtrip ahead.

Since Christ lives in you through the power of His Spirit, you have everything you need for this life of living for God. 2 Peter 1:3 says, *"His divine power has given us everything we need for life and godliness through our knowledge of him who called us by his own glory and goodness."*

There are two things that will help you live in this reality. The first is faith. Hebrews 11:6 says, *"Without faith it is impossible to please God."* It takes faith to become a Christian and it takes faith to live as the Christian you have become.

In the same way that you trust (aka have faith) in Jesus to save you from your sins, you have to trust that He can live through you, empowering you to do what you could never do on your own. Consider this. When you become a believer, it's true that you do not see the physical reality that your name is written in the Book of Life and that one day you will be in heaven with God forever. But you believe it to be true and you live as though it is. You count on it. In the same way, you may not see the physical reality that Jesus lives in you, but you need to believe it, count on it and then live as though it were true.

The second thing that will help you is to learn how to tell whether it's Jesus living through you or whether it's just your same old sinful nature. In order to learn the difference, it helps to know what Jesus' life looked like back when He walked the earth 2000 years ago. This will help you better know what becoming like Him might look like today.

This is one of the many reasons why you need to spend time reading the Bible, learning from the gospels about how Jesus lived—what He was like in person, what things He cared about and what things He focused on.

For instance, you'll see that Jesus was compassionate as you read about His life. You, too, should strive to be compassionate, caring for others, striving to do it according to Jesus' strength through you. You'll see that Jesus spent time building deeply into the lives of others, so you should too, by His power in you. I could go on at length, but I think you get the point. Each of us should search the Bible to see for ourselves how Jesus lived back then, in order to keep us focused now.

One good passage that sums up much of what you should be like as you follow Jesus and allow Him to live through you is Galatians 5:22-23: *"The fruit of the Spirit is love, joy, peace, patience, kindness, goodness, faithfulness, gentleness and self-control."* You start to get the picture that "following Jesus" may take you the rest of your life to perfect—and probably longer. ☺

I would even encourage you to memorize that passage. And then as you go about your daily life, ask the question, *am I doing this in "love"?* Or when something makes you sad and you're hurting, ask *do I still sense the "joy" of Christ in the midst of this situation right now?* Maybe there is a trial you are going through and it is freaking you out, *is God's "peace" greater than the storm?* Or maybe a certain person always makes you mad, how do you respond, *is it with the "kindness" of God?*

When you find that your life is not ripe with the "fruit of the Spirit" and you are not living like Jesus, don't just try and force it and fake it. Ask Jesus to help you do what you cannot do on your own. This is what it means to be dependent upon Him.

The coolest part of this whole depending on God for the strength-to-live-for-Him thing is that Jesus Himself lived this way. You see, Jesus even being God lived in total dependence upon God the Father. In John 5:19 He explained it this way, *"I tell you the truth, the Son"*—referring to Himself—*"can do nothing by himself, he can do only what he sees his Father doing, because whatever the Father does, the Son also does."*

In His every thought and action Jesus depended upon the Father. He unleashed the endless power and potential we have fully available to us if we live plugged into God's power!

Jesus is our model and through faith He also becomes our method, the very means through which we accomplish His call.

7

SNOWBOARDING AND FISHING

There is joy in the journey.

"'*Come follow me,*' *Jesus said,* '*and I will make you fishers of men*'" (Matthew 4:19).

Becoming a "fisher of men" is not just something to add on top of a person's already full life. This is an entire shift of focus, a new way of doing life all together.

For Jesus, this is what it means to follow.

Honestly, when I first heard about becoming a fisher of people, I had no clue what it meant, plus I don't even like regular fishing. Every time I would go fishing with my dad growing up, it meant me taking a nap in the boat. Fishing would always involve getting up so early that I was pretty sure God wasn't even awake. Then I'd miss my morning cartoons to go float out in the middle of the ocean, which sounds to me more like something people who are stranded do. If we did catch fish, it only meant that I would have the amazing privilege of cleaning the fish later, ripping out the intestines, getting covered in guts and smelling like fish for the next two days.

So what's fishing got to do with Jesus' call to follow?

I guess I am still not fully sure.

But it is interesting that these guys were already fishermen when Jesus called them to fish for people instead of flounders.

These guys had worked hard at their previous job and now Jesus is tapping into their experience as fishermen and relating it to what it means to "follow Him." It's not like He said that their old way of living was completely useless, having no value if they became Christ followers. It's almost like He was saying the exact opposite, showing us that He can use the things of our past as we live out His call on our lives in the present.

This is where it gets a little difficult to define, because this will look different for different people. For me, it meant that I actually had to make a clean break from my past. There were so many toxic behaviors, choices and surrounding pressures that I had to get away from in order for me to really follow Jesus and "fish for men." But once I made the break with my past lifestyle, I began to find that some of the things from my past began to be my greatest tools for ministry in the present.

These were just little random pieces of my past, but it was so cool for me to see how God could use them for His purpose. For instance, I used to drive a semi truck for a beer company as a delivery guy. The sweet thing was that the beer company paid for me to get my commercial driver's license (CDL), enabling me to drive big rigs. This special kind of license can cost up to $5,000. When I came to the Torchbearers Bible School, they needed someone who had a CDL to drive shuttles for the youth groups that would visit. Thanks to the beer company, I can now be the youth group shuttle driver.

From beer truck driver to youth group shuttle driver, Jesus doesn't waste experiences.

Even in the initial process of coming to Torchbearers to go to school I had to come up with money for tuition, room and board. So I asked friends and family members to help, and as gracious as people were in giving me money, I still hadn't raised the entire amount. But a couple days before school started, I sold a car that I had bought with drug money and that is essentially how I paid for my tuition…with drug money!

Or here's another one. **My greatest passion in all of life before I became a Christian was**

snowboarding. At the Bible School, not only did I get to snowboard, but it was like I got to snowboard for Jesus. When youth groups would come and visit, I got to take them out to the mountain and teach them how to snowboard, but I also got to teach them about Jesus at the same time!

But the crazy part was that when I first came to Torchbearers, I actually felt like God wanted me to put my passion for snowboarding on the backburner. So the first year, I only snowboarded 20 times. I know this may sound like a lot to some of you. But I was used to snowboarding 60+ days per year and that was when I lived four hours, roundtrip, away from the mountain. When I moved to the Bible School, I could snowboard in my backyard, but I only went 20 times! It was like I was giving it up so God could get my priorities straight and show me the real purpose for my having the ability to snowboard.

Once God became my number one, it was like He then gave me back snowboarding as a tool I could use for Him. I started competing and began to win medals, clothing and other sweet gear. I even got featured in a couple small snowboard films. But that was not my focus or goal. My goal was to share the love of God. I began to pray every day before I would go snowboarding, not for safety, but for opportunities to tell peeps about Jesus. My favorite days were competition days. Because all the younger kids would see me doing practice runs, or wearing my competition bib, and it opened up opportunities to talk to them about Jesus.

[Always looking for opportunities to tell peeps about Jesus!]

I'm now part of a ministry called "Snowboarders and Skiers For Christ" (sfc-usa.com) and I get to reach out to the snowboard community with the gospel in super fun ways. They do Bible studies, snowboard waxing parties, competitions, camps, clothing, stickers and just recently I was in their snowboard film *Serious Fun*.

It's kinda like being a "fisher of men," but snowboard style—snowboarding for men, not for medals.

God has always been in the business of using past experiences for His present purposes. I mean, just look at the dude in the Old Testament named David. David grew up as a shepherd boy, taking care of the family flock. Psalm 78:70-72 talks about God's call on David's life this way,

> *He chose David his servant, and took him from the sheep pens; from tending the sheep he brought him to be the shepherd of his people… and David shepherded them with integrity of heart; with skillful hands he led them.*

David was a shepherd boy for years. It could have seemed like he was wasting those years out there all alone in the fields with smelly sheep. But as David remained faithful, God's bigger purposes became clearer, for God chose him to be King over all of Israel. And God used his times in the field with the sheep to prepare him to rule in the castle over God's people. God's call on David's life was for a purpose.

And Jesus' call on your life is for a purpose, too.

Maybe you feel like you are living an insignificant life, wasting away your years. Maybe it seems as though God could never use you for something great. Well, let me tell you, God doesn't waste experiences. So make the most of the place you are in and give God all you've got, 'cause you never know what He is preparing you for. God doesn't waste experiences and neither should you. You may need that experience tomorrow.

And like the disciples, you're called to fish, not for money, wealth or personal gain, but for the lives of people. This is a call to become like Jesus and rescue the lost.

Jesus' life was consumed with this pursuit. In Luke 19:10 He says, *"The Son of Man* (referring to Himself) *came to seek and to save what was lost* (referring to us)." His purpose on this earth, given to Him by God, was to set the captives free from their bondage of sin, bringing people back into relationship with their heavenly Father.

This is our purpose too, well, minus the whole dying on the cross to pay for the sin of the world part. Jesus says in John 20:21, *"As the Father has sent me, I am sending you."* God the Father sent Jesus Christ into this world to open the way of salvation, and now Jesus sends us as fishers of men, to tell others about Him, the One who is the way for salvation.

This is the full call of Jesus. To love God with everything you've got, and then to love others with that same reckless love.

We would all say that we love our friends and that we would do just about anything for them. If that's true, then we should do the *most* important thing for them, which is sharing with them about the love of God. If we hold back from them the good news of the gospel, then we are actually exhibiting the exact opposite of love.

Why wouldn't we want to tell our friends about the gospel? Think about all that God has done for us, all of who God is to us. Think about the beauty of creation—mountains, rivers, sunsets, the ocean and lakes. How much more amazing is the God who created all of that? And we have the privilege of telling people about this God and His love for them. Not only the beauty of God, His majesty and glory, but also how He satisfies our souls, bringing happiness to our hearts and fulfilling our every longing.

This is a God worth boasting about!

So follow Jesus and use your energy, talents, abilities, hobbies, interests and time to pursue others in love. Be willing to risk whatever it takes to share the good news of Jesus with others.

This is not going to be easy, but it's going to be worth it.

I actually have some staples that I keep in my Bible to remind me of this very truth. You see, awhile back I was on a surfing trip in California with a good buddy when I took a gnarly little wipeout. In the midst of going through the ocean's tumble cycle, I ended up getting bashed in the head with my surfboard. When the ocean finally felt I'd had enough and let me up to breathe, I noticed I was feeling a bit funny. I wasn't sure if it was from the lack of oxygen or because I had just gotten smashed in the head by a giant fiberglass board.

[Surfing is my favorite sport!]

So I gave my head a good little shake, trying to get the "cobwebs" out. As I did, blood scattered across the ocean's surface. All of a sudden I realized I was bleeding profusely from the back of my head. As I looked at the pool of blood surrounding me, I instantly thought…SHARK!

The buddy with me was a former college linebacker. When he saw the blood, he rushed to help me, parting the waters like Moses. He threw me over his shoulder and rescued me to safety.

I ended up getting 12 staples in the back of my head. And they used a staple gun just like what you get from the hardware store! When I got them removed, I asked if I could keep them. These are the staples I keep in my Bible to remind me that the Christian life is a little dangerous, but it is worth it.

My favorite sport still to this day is surfing, despite—or maybe even because of—the difficulty and risk involved.

There is even greater risk involved in following Jesus. But it is even more worth it. **When you embrace His call to become a fisher of men, you will experience some of the greatest letdowns, but also some of the greatest joys.**

We get a glimpse of what this looks like in Luke 10:17 when Jesus sent out a group of His followers on a "fishing trip," preaching and proclaiming the good news of God. This involved great risk, and even greater reward. When this group of 72 came back, it says that they returned with "joy." They found joy in rescuing others and doing what God had called them to. The same is true for us.

There is joy in the journey.

Will you accept this mission to become a "fisher of men" and begin seeking to partner with God in the rescuing of your friends from the grip of sin and Satan?

Start today. Start by making the most of where you are right now. Step up to the risk. It's worth it!

8
GOD'S AGENTS OF LOVE

**True love is willing to risk whatever it takes
for the greater good.**

I used to think video games were lame—thought
they were a waste of life.

I have one friend who totaled up the hours he
played video games during his sophomore, junior
and senior year and it came to 4,000 hours.

FOUR THOUSAND hours. Just think about it.
If you were to sleep eight hours a day and then
do absolutely nothing else other than play video
games—that's no bathroom breaks, shower breaks
or anything, just straight gaming—for one thing,
you would be really stinky. But it would amount to
almost nine straight months of just playing video
games. Nine months of your life gone.

So I have never been much of a gamer, especially
by the standard of this particular buddy. But that
was before what I'm about to tell you happened.

I had another friend who got his first Wii awhile
back. He would not stop talking about it. Then I
went to stay with him in California for a week of
surfing. Each night as we were all dead tired and

heading to bed, he would bust out the Wii. He was like a spider monkey all jacked up on Mountain Dew. He would be jumping, laughing and going crazy as he played his new Wii.

After the first couple days of this, I thought, *this looks kinda fun.* Before I knew it, I too was getting serious about some Wii action. By the end of the trip, I was hooked. Even more than being tired

[During the filming of *GOSPEL Journey Maui,* I got to share both my love for Jesus and my love of surfing with the cast.]

from the all day surf sessions, I was tired from staying up too late playing Wii every night. His passion and love for the Wii wore off on me.

If that can happen with something like video games, then imagine how your love for the God of the universe, who actually satisfies your soul, can rub off on others.

And get this. **People will experience your love for God by the way you love them.**

Never forget this as you reach out to others and point them to the Father by expressing His immense love towards them. And always remember that people are not projects. Each individual is a person created uniquely by God, in His image, and is someone Jesus Christ gave His life for when He died on the cross. Your goal is not to go around "fixing" people, as though they are just another task for you to complete. You are to love them.

I'm not saying it's always easy. But Jesus actually commands it. Check this out: *"My command is this: Love each other as I have loved you. Greater love has no one than this: to lay down one's life for one's friends"* (John 15:12-13, NIV, 2011).

You must be willing to give of your time, energy, money and whatever else it might take to love others with a radical love. You must be willing to lay down your very life for those you are trying to reach.

One way you can do this is by going out of your way to help others out. This can be something as small as reaching out a hand in a football game to help up the opposing team member you just tackled. It can mean sharing your lunch with someone who forgot theirs or letting someone go first in line. It can be offering to pay for lunch, getting someone a gift or sitting next to the loner. It's basically about putting the needs and wellbeing of others first.

And sometimes, laying down your life means being bold enough to risk an awkward conversation. It can be scary trying to talk to people about God. What if they don't like what we say? What if it offends them?

Love is willing to risk whatever it takes for the greater good.

What if they get mad enough to not want to be your friend? What if what you say causes them to hate you? Surely God wouldn't want you to go so far as to lose a friend, because that wouldn't be loving, or would it?

Jesus has something to say about this type of situation and it's pretty interesting. In Matthew 10:37-39, when Jesus sends out His 12 disciples on what seems like a missions trip, He concludes His sendoff speech by saying,

> *"Anyone who loves their father or mother more than me is not worthy of me; anyone who loves their son or daughter more than me is not worthy of me. Whoever does not take up their cross and follow me is not worthy of me. Whoever finds their life will lose it, and whoever loses their life for my sake will find it"* (NIV, 2011).

It seems like Jesus is saying if we want to truly follow Him, we have to be willing to risk not only the things we value the most, but the relationships we value most as well.

Our love for others is important, but our love for God has to be even greater. We must not place our earthly relationships above our heavenly relationship. We must never seek approval from friends above approval from God. **Our love for God must be our greatest motivator and should be what fuels us to risk sharing with our friends.**

If we truly do love our friends, then we will be willing to risk whatever it takes. Because we see that even more than how they may need our love, they need the love and forgiveness of a heavenly Father.

Our love for others should not be with expectation of return either. We must realize that Christ-like, sacrificial love extends grace when others are under-appreciative, unthankful and even sometimes take advantage of us.

Romans 5:8 says, *"God demonstrates his own love for us in this: While we were still sinners, Christ died for us."* The only way we can give away that kind of sacrificial love is if we ourselves have received it—like it says in John 15:12, *"Love each other as I have loved you."* So we must continually open ourselves up to God, allowing Him to fill us with rivers of His love, because then and only then, can we overflow with His love to others.

We need to point them to the One who is love. And the gospel is the greatest demonstration of His love, so it's vital that we share it over and over. It is the heartbeat of Christianity. We need to live it and give it!

Like 1 John 3:16 says, *"This is how we know what love is: Jesus Christ laid down his life for us. And we ought to lay down our lives for our brothers."*

**In this quest, our hearts are going to need to be
continually filled up with the love of God, so that
we then have the ability to pour it out to others.**

That's why God tells us we need to be continually
filled by His Holy Spirit, for it is the power of
God in us that gives us passion and enables us
to live for Him. So we need to daily submit and
surrender to Him, asking for strength to overcome
our sins and struggles and for the power to live
and love like Him.

Think of it like this. The difference between a
swamp and a river is "flow." A swamp is stagnant
and dead. Sure, new water comes in, but it has
nowhere to go, so it only gets stinky and stagnant.
A river on the other hand, is continually being
refreshed by new water pouring into it and it never
stops flowing out, either. You can dam it up, but
it will just create deep lakes and reservoirs until it
eventually overflows again, because it is continually
being refilled and it must flow. Both are being filled,
but only the river continues to pour out as well,
therefore it never becomes stagnant and stinky.

If we are going to grow and not become
stagnant and stinky, we too must overflow with
God's love to others.

Like a river constantly flowing, we too need to be continually poured into by God so we can pour into others. As God's passion and strength grows in us, it will flow out of us. And like passion for Wii rubbing off on me, our passion for God can rub off on others, because they will not just hear about our love for God, they will experience it through us.

9
LIVE IT AND GIVE IT

**Let's live lives that wear the title Christian
like a badge of honor.**

I love going to the skate park to skate, but even more, to tell people about Jesus.

Skateboarding for me has become less about learning new tricks and more about communicating the love of God. Maybe that's why I am stuck still doing tricks from the 80's and the kids at the park have started calling me "Grandpa!" I tell them, "I may be Grandpa, but even worse than being called it is getting schooled by a grandpa!" Then I bust out my 80's tricks.

I remember one time specifically when I was telling this group of kids about Jesus and they were actually listening! I started getting all excited. And the more excited I got, the louder I got. From the other side of the skate park, this other group of kids heard me. One was this dude with a mohawk about a foot tall, dressed in all black with piercings all over his face and a snarl on his mouth. Mohawk dude walked over to our group, planted himself right into the center of the group, looked me right in the eyes and said, "I........hate......Christians."

You could have heard a pin drop in the skate park at that moment. Everyone went totally silent, wondering what's Jesus boy going to do.

So I said the first thing that came to my mind, which isn't always a good thing. My dad says I have diarrhea of the mouth and constipation of the brain. So out came, "Me too." I don't know what I was thinking, apparently I wasn't. So I just started praying, praying like I had never prayed before.

Then I was like, "I mean, I used to hate Christians, because I thought they were just hypocrites."

This set mohawk man off!

Mohawk dude started raising his voice and getting ticked, ranting, "Yeah, stinking hypocrites, they are always acting like they have it all together, being all goodie goodie and telling me my life is messed up. They always judge me and look down on me because I'm different. They always pretend to be better than me. Well, I know the truth, they are just as messed up. They can take their stinking religion and their Jesus…" He continued on in a ramble of swear words, trying to express his frustration.

After he was done, I knew it was my opening. "You know who also got mad at hypocrites?"

"Who?"

"Jesus."

"What?!"

I thought this might be my only chance, so I went for it. "Yeah, you see, there were these people who were supposed to be like God's representatives here on earth. They were meant to help the hurting, seek after the lost and repair the broken. But instead, they missed what it actually meant to be God's people and they lived as hypocrites, judging others instead of helping them. So when Jesus came along, these people actually got mad at Him because He was always hanging with the down and out."

He hadn't stopped me yet so I kept going, "If Jesus was here today, I bet He too would be ticked at the Christians today who are living as hypocrites. Jesus didn't come for those who think they have it all together, but for dudes like you and me who know we are messed up. It was the outcast who wanted to hang out with Jesus, because He loved them as they were and offered them hope to change. The hypocrites ended up being the ones who crucified Jesus."

Well, that didn't go as I thought, because mohawk man just got even madder. "What! They killed Jesus!" He was almost yelling at the top of his lungs now.

In my last-ditch effort to calm the guy down I said, "Don't worry, man, Jesus had the last laugh, 'cause three days later He rose from the dead. And through a relationship with Him—not a religious following of rules—but a relationship, you and I both can be united with Jesus and experience a relationship with Him. We can experience what we were made for— the worship of God—and we can be with Him forever in heaven."

"Oh," he said. Then he walked away.

Then I peed my pants. Just a little—well, not really—but it was so intense, I didn't know what to do. Everybody just went back to skating.

[I love training teenagers to share the GOSPEL Journey Message at Dare 2 Share Conferences.]

How to Explain the Gospel

When telling our friends about Jesus it's good to talk about being in a relationship with Him and about how He is about more than rules and regulations. Find creative ways to make much of Jesus. And be prepared to communicate the fullness of the message of the gospel in a clear, concise way that people can understand without leaving out any important parts.

Here's one approach, called the GOSPEL Journey Message, that helps me make sure I'm not leaving anything important out. Because sharing the gospel is kinda like taking someone on a journey. But rather than starting at point "A" and moving on to point "B," you start at "G" and then journey through the rest of the letters, "-OSPEL," stopping at each point along the way in your conversation.

Here are the six points along the way:

God created us to be with Him.
Our sins separate us from God.
Sins cannot be removed by good deeds.
Paying the price for sin, Jesus died and rose again.
Everyone who trusts in Him alone has eternal life.
Life with Jesus starts now and lasts forever.

Personally, I've memorized these points and now I can share them confidently whenever I get into a conversation about Jesus (like with mohawk dude). Using this approach, helps me make sure that I'm covering the important parts of His message. And trust me, the more you become familiar with it, the more natural it will be for you to communicate these truths with confidence and creativity.

You can also see a sweet video called *Life in 6 Words* featuring my good friend, Jason Petty ("Propaganda"), explaining these six points. Check it out at Lifein6Words.com and maybe even use the video to share the gospel with others.

I tried to kind of follow mohawk dude around as we skated for the rest of the day, and kept building the relationship. I asked him questions about his life, told him his tricks were sick and encouraged him any chance I had.

As I was getting ready to leave, one of mohawk dude's little followers came over to me and said, "Are you going to come back and skate with us again?" It was like he didn't want me to go. This got me pumped, maybe God was using me. "For sure, man!" I exclaimed, maybe sounding a little too excited. Then the little dude actually hugged me!

As I went to get into my car, from the far side of the skate park I heard mohawk man yell, "Don't I get a hug too?"

My eyes lit up and I ran to him like a long lost brother—a brother from another mother. As I gave him a big ole bear hug, I thought to myself, "Who would have ever imagined that the love of God could be displayed at a skate park even to those most resistant?"

Like I said before, I could identify with mohawk man, because before I became a Christian, I thought all Christians were hypocrites too. They pretended like they were all goodie goodie, but I could see they were just as messed up as I was.

Sometimes one of the biggest things that contributes to people not wanting to follow Jesus is His "followers." I can't tell you how many times I have heard people say, "I like Jesus, just not Christians," or "I like Jesus, just not the Church." I have even seen bumper stickers that say, "Lord, save us from your followers."

When I first became a believer, I felt like there was so much baggage that came along with being a "Christian" that I decided I wouldn't call myself a "Christian." I would call myself a "Christ follower." After all, that's what Christians are supposed to be, right? The Greek word for Christian is actually *Christianos,* which literally means "follower of Christ."

But then one day I was reading through the book of Acts and came to verse 11:26 where it says, *"The disciples were called Christians first at Antioch."* I did some more study and found out that the use of the word "Christian" was actually started by the non-Christians. It was most likely first used as a way to make fun of the disciples, mocking them by calling them "little Christs." But the early Christians started using the term as a badge of honor, not of shame, and they changed the meaning.

I started thinking, what if we could do the same? What if we decided to fight the common label of "hypocrite Christian" and we began to redefine Christianity in the eyes of non-believers? Rather than abandon our spiritual heritage, what if we clung to it and showed people what real Christianity is?

What if we lived lives that wear the title "Christian" like a badge of honor?

But this means we actually have to work at becoming more like Jesus. In fact, He tells His followers in Luke 6:40 that a fully trained disciple will be like their teacher.

So our goal must be to be like Jesus.

To be like Christ is a pretty lofty aim, it seems pretty unattainable. And, well, I guess it kind of is, seeing as Jesus was perfect and all. 'Cause if you're like me, you're far from perfect. So maybe all the non-Christians are right. In one sense, we are all hypocrites, because we claim to be "Christians," aka "little Christs," but we fall far short.

Maybe instead of running from the accusation that we are hypocrites, we should actually embrace it. Because they're right, we don't add up. When we pretend to have it all together, it's only a matter of time before we fail and our true colors show how far from perfect we truly are. That's when non-believers feel lied to and see us as a bunch of fakes. Who can blame them for thinking we're hypocrites?

So what if rather than pretending like we have it all together, we acknowledge that we're sorry we aren't a clearer picture of Christ on earth? All the while trying to increasingly live in the Spirit's power and become more like Jesus. Maybe then our friends would see that we struggle too, and that just like them, we are continually in need of a Savior.

After all, being a follower of Jesus requires the humility to acknowledge our sin. The Apostle Paul went as far as to say, *"I will boast all the more gladly about my weaknesses, so that Christ's power may rest on me"* (2 Corinthians 12:9).

This doesn't give us an excuse to just sit back and accept our sin. We should go to battle against it with the strength of God, just like a UFC cage fighter trains with laser focus, strengthening his mind and body for battle against his opponent. We too need to train ourselves to be godly (1 Timothy 4:7) in order to overcome our sin. We do this by depending on the power of the Holy Spirit to come into our lives and transform us through Bible reading, studying, memorizing and staying continually connected to Him. We get powered up by spending time in prayer, like Jude 1:20 tells us, *"build yourselves up in your most holy faith and pray in the Holy Spirit."*

We need to *"throw off everything that hinders"* (Hebrews12:1), laying aside the things that are holding us back. There might even be things in our lives that aren't necessarily bad, but just don't build us up. We need to get rid of these, just like a fighter controls his diet by eliminating certain foods that normal people eat in order to bring his best to every fight.

This passage in Hebrews continues on by saying: *"Let us fix our eyes on Jesus, the author and perfecter of our faith."* **When fighting against sin, it's critical that we train ourselves to focus on Jesus. He will help us in our struggle.**

But even as we go to battle with our sin, we will still fall short. When this happens, remember that it provides an opportunity to explain God's grace. As we're real with others about our failures, it gives us the chance to explain God's love and mercy.

Just recently I was talking with a student who had become a Christian years ago, but had fallen back into temptation and had lived the party life for the last couple years. Still, God hadn't given up on her and had brought her back to a full on surrendered life. She wanted so badly to start sharing with her party friends because she loved them, but she felt so ashamed and knew she was a hypocrite. She ended up just avoiding those friends, because she felt she couldn't face them.

She and I talked through this idea of actually using the fact that she had lived hypocritically to point her friends toward Jesus' forgiveness. She was scared, but she went for it. And God used her in huge ways. Her friends stopped putting her on a "Christian pedestal" and started seeing her as a normal teenager, with normal struggles, but one who had found hope and forgiveness in Jesus.

Let's strive to live holy lives with all of God's strength, but let's also be open enough to admit our faults.

And remember, you don't have to wait until you're perfect to share Jesus with others. You just have to love them and then jump in and look for ways to point them toward God.

10
BEANS AND CAMPING

RECKLESS

Do you think Jesus ever laughed at a fart?

I have a lot of memories from my time as a student at the Torchbearers School living in a dorm packed in with bunk beds and six smelly dudes. As though it were seared in with a hot iron, one of those vivid memories is the "modern warfare night," and no, I'm not talking about the *Call of Duty* video game.

My roommates and I had just gotten back from stuffing ourselves on Mexican food. Yup, lots of the musical fruit. Needless to say, our room became like a warzone for chemical warfare. The stench was so bad that it felt like the paint would peel off the walls and my eyes would burn up. As repulsive as it was, for some reason with every explosion, we continued to laugh. Let's be honest, farts are funny.

I mean, we've all experienced that time in class where everybody is supposed to be silent and then, all of a sudden, someone lets one rip. Because of the plastic seats, it's amplified as though through a loudspeaker. The guilty gasser always tries to play it cool like nothing happened—unless it was intentional, in which case they try to pass it off on some innocent kid sitting nearby. Meanwhile, the entire class breaks out into uncontrollable laughter. Even the meanest of teachers can't hold back the inevitable smile, or maybe even outburst of laughter.

In the midst of the bombs being dropped in our room one of my friends stopped for a second, fanning the air that was thick enough you could grab it, and said, "Do you think Jesus ever laughed at a fart?"

At first this only caused us to laugh harder, envisioning one of the disciples asking Jesus to "pull his finger," while the other disciples waited to see if He would go for it. The laughter fully erupted as another friend asked, "Did Jesus ever let a little stinker?"

Our halfway serious, halfway joking questions turned into an hour long conversation. One of the points brought into consideration for this highly theological discussion was that Jesus was essentially on a three year camping trip with 12 other dudes.

I don't know how many of you have been camping, but for those who have, you know that when camping with a group, not much is hidden. There for sure had to have been a time when at least

[Me and my buddies rockin' it on the slopes.]

Judas let one sneak by. And I think we can assume that the other dudes would have laughed. It's like a natural human reaction to laugh at tooters. Did Jesus?

Our conversation led us past the "cutting of cheese" and on to the character of Christ and what it means that Jesus was both fully God and fully human. Whether or not Jesus laughed at the disciples when they had a little bottom burp, we may never know. But either way, that night turned out to be a pretty legit conversation as we explored some things about Jesus that most people don't discuss.

We laughed at times till tears were coming out of our eyes and at other times it got so real you could hear a pin drop in the room as we sat in silence contemplating just how amazing God truly is.

It was fun to focus on Jesus with friends. And that is how it should be.

Jesus was not some somber, gloomy, boring guy. He was interesting, exciting to be around and maybe even funny. The religious people hated Him, but the sinners constantly wanted to be around Him. Something about Him drew crowds of thousands to come listen to Him. One of His first recorded miracles happened at a party (John 2:1-11). Yet Jesus is often pictured as the ultimate "killjoy," always trying to keep people from doing anything fun. But in this case of His first miracle, the real Jesus actually helped keep the party going.

Jesus said stuff that was hilarious too. Well, at least to His original audience, some of the stuff He said was pretty funny. It doesn't always seem that funny to us because we are reading it 2000 years later in a different language and culture than it originally happened.

But think about Matthew 7:4 where Jesus said, *"How can you say to your brother, 'Let me take the speck out of your eye,' when all the time there is a plank in your own eye?"* This is funny in the context of what is happening. Or when Jesus talked about how a rich man entering heaven is like a camel passing through the eye of a needle—even the thought of it is ridiculous. It's humorous.

The conversation in our room that night went from guys just being guys to us having a super encouraging and challenging discussion. And this is an example of how to look for openings in everyday life where you can point people toward Jesus so they can get to know Him better.

When you're hanging out with friends who are non-Christians, you should be thinking about how you can use your time with them to talk about or show just how awesome Jesus is. You're in their life to help them in their journey, drawing them closer to a relationship with Him. And you can have fun doing it.

It's not like you need to all of a sudden stop doing all the stuff you love or that you need to get a whole new set of vocabulary so you can talk like some holy roller. Although again, there may be stuff that you shouldn't be doing or words you shouldn't be using. But movies, video games, sports, hobbies, music, Facebook and yes, even farts, can be used to help you point your non-Christian friends to Jesus, if they are used in the right way with the right mindset (aka evangelism).

This can be simple stuff. Evangelism doesn't have to be this nerve-racking time where you feel all this pressure to make your friends Christians. That's God's job, actually. You're just there to point them toward Him.

[Having fun at the ocean on a hot summer day.]

So let's say you're out hanging with your friends at the lake, having fun on a hot summer day. Everybody is talking about how much they love being at the lake and being in the sun and you say, "Yeah, how amazing is it that God created all of this!" They respond by saying, "You actually believe all that?" You follow up with, "I guess I just don't have enough faith to believe it's all here by random chance."

You may not lay out the gospel in every conversation, but you are showing your friends that your relationship with God is not something hidden and secret. It is something you are proud of and want to put on display, because you truly believe that God is that great.

You are showing them what it's like to love God.

Or it may be as simple as giving God the credit for a job well done. Let's say you get a good grade on a test or get named MVP at a volleyball tournament. Or maybe someone compliments you by saying you're always happy or you're a really nice person. Find a way to give God the credit. Here's an example. Since I became a Christian, people are like, "Zane, are you always smiling?" First, I say, "No, I too have bad days." (You don't want to lie or give false pictures of the Christian life being all rosy.) Then I say, "But yeah, I guess I do smile a lot. I guess God has just given me a lot to smile about."

Depending on how they respond, that might be all I say. **I like to think that sharing with my friends is a marathon, not a sprint.**

It's not that you avoid sharing the entire message; it's just that you don't need to do it in every single conversation. But you always want to be open and ready, so when those times do come (and they always do, if you're looking for them), you can go for it.

With your Christian friends, pointing your conversations toward God is part of building each other up in your walk with Jesus. Think of how you can "sharpen" each other. Proverbs 27:17 says, *"As iron sharpens iron, so one person sharpens another."* How can you challenge others and be challenged yourself to grow in your relationship with God and in your passion to share Him with others.

Our conversation that night could have stayed centered on who had the mightiest blast of flatulence, but instead, one of the guys turned it to Jesus. Proving that just about any conversation can be turned toward Jesus.

But doing this is going to take two things: time spent with your friends and time spent with God.

'Cause how can you point people toward Jesus if you don't know Him well yourself?

So it's really important that you spend time with God. Jesus modeled how much of a priority this needs to be for us. He was constantly sneaking away by Himself to spend time with God the Father, even waking up early in the morning or staying up late so He could make it happen. Sure, it's true that we can talk to God anytime, anywhere, even in the midst of a crowded room or a busy schedule. But it is important for us to take times that are set apart to be alone with God, even if it means taking just 15 minutes before school or heading to bed early so you can read and pray before your head hits the pillow.

Alone Time with God

Jesus placed great importance on being alone with the Father. We should too. Here are some examples of what this looked like for Him.

Refreshment
Mark 1:35: *"Very early in the morning, while it was still dark, Jesus got up, left the house and went off to a solitary place, where he prayed."*

Empowering for impactful ministry
Matthew 4:1: Jesus went out into the desert for 40 days and 40 nights before the start of His public ministry.

Comfort in hard times
Matthew 14:13: When Jesus heard the bad news about the death of His friend, He immediately went out in a boat alone, seeking comfort in the arms of His heavenly Father.

Refocusing in good times
Luke 5:15-16: As Jesus became more popular He sought out even more times alone with the Father.

Guidance before big decisions
Luke 6:12-13: Jesus went out and prayed all night before choosing His 12 disciples.

Strength for difficult things ahead
Luke 22:39-46: Before the crucifixion Jesus even invited others to pray, as well, while

He went off to be alone with the Father in anticipation of the cross to come.

So no matter what your situation, spend time alone with your heavenly Father and pour your heart out to Him.

And just like Jesus did when He used things that were part of His everyday life to share spiritual truths—fishing, farming and even weeds—you want to look for little opportunities to bring the jokes, games, movies and conversations back to God.

The better you personally know God, the easier and more natural this will be. Even to the point of being able to transition from eating too many beans to talking about what matters most in life—Jesus.

Colossians 4:5-6 says it this way, *"Use your heads as you live and work among outsiders…Make the most of every opportunity. Be gracious in your speech. The goal is to bring out the best in others in a conversation, not put them down, not cut them out"* (The Message).

11
NO LONERS

**As disciples of Jesus,
discipling others is not optional.**

I can remember when I first got invited to go speak
at these events called Dare 2 Share. At the time,
the conferences would reach about 50,000 people
over the course of a tour. A couple of the events
were so big they had to be held in sporting arenas,
reaching crowds of up to 8,000 students. And I got
invited to be one of the speakers.

Needless to say, I thought I was going to poop
my pants.

I mean, I was excited and all, but I was also
freaked out! I was not some great speaker who
had experience with these types of things. I'd had
opportunities to teach and speak before, but it
was mainly at my little Torchbearers Bible School
where we averaged 30 students. Every once in
awhile I'd get asked to speak at youth group
retreats with about 60 students and even that
always freaked me out.

To be honest, I am always freaked out when I
have to speak in front of a group of people, even
still today! It turns out I am not the only one. I

searched online and most people are more afraid of public speaking than they are of dying.

I remember clearly the first time I ever spoke at a youth group. I got so nervous I started sweating. Then I got nervous that I was sweating and the minor glistening perspiration turned into open floodgates of sweat rushing like a river pouring down my face. I must have looked like a fat man in a sauna. Sweat even began to run down my back and I think one drip made it all the way down to my shoe. It was not a pleasant sight. I was so freaked out that I clung to the music stand where my notes were with a white-knuckle grip as though my life depended on it.

Afterwards, the youth pastor came up and said he thought I did good because he could see my passion!

So when the invitation to travel and speak on this Dare 2 Share tour came, I was totally freaked out to a whole new level. I had no clue what I was going to do. It seemed like the spiritual answer would be to pray about it. So I decided I needed an army of people to pray about it. Just in case my prayers weren't enough, I sent out prayer letters to everyone I knew, even the atheists. I figured maybe when they heard I would be speaking in front of thousands of teenagers it might just be enough of a crisis to cause them to cry out to God too.

In the prayer letter, I put things like, "Pray that God will speak through me." I mean, He spoke through a donkey in Numbers 22 and I figured He could do it again, because sometimes I feel like a donkey. But then I also put, "Pray that I don't poop my pants on stage." Hey, I was just covering the basics. I ended up bringing Depends diapers (which are actually old people diapers), just in case. Seriously. OK, I didn't end up using them, but I did bring them to every event and they reminded me to "depend" on the Lord. ☺

Even though I was freaked out, God did some awesome stuff in and through me. I was super humbled to see how God could use even me. Even when I was ready to mess my shorts, God could still speak through me.

But then partway through the Dare 2 Share tour, they decided that they wanted to make a "Zane" t-shirt. Now this is where it got weird. A shirt with my face on it? That would freak anybody out. Through the process, they came up with all sorts of designs, but the final was actually designed by my pastor, Doug Horch, and it had a picture of me acting like a goofball (not much new there), but then the tagline was going to say "Follow Me."

This freaked me out! I don't want students following me, I want them following Jesus! Who am I to say "follow me," as if I have any clue about what I am doing. I mean, isn't that the most conceited, bigheaded, arrogant thing a person could say? Unless, of course, if you are Jesus. And then you actually are worthy of being followed.

I told Doug how uncomfortable I was with it, expressing how once the shirt was produced, I couldn't take it back and it would be out there forever. This would mean I would have to live a life that was worth following.

I will never forget what Doug told me. "Zane," he said, "just because we make the shirt, doesn't change anything. This is what every Christian should be able to say. 'Follow me.'"

Wow, so true. Think about it. The whole premise of this book is about how Jesus called people to follow Him in order to find out what it looked like to live for God.

And a primary way Jesus did this was by making disciples. **If we are to "follow Him," then we too should make disciples. We do this by mentoring others and showing them what it looks like to live for God.** We have a part to play in other's lives and that's to help them grow up in Christ.

In fact, making disciples was central to Jesus' final charge to His followers. He made it as clear as can be in Matthew 28:18-20 when He said,

> *"All authority in heaven and on earth has been given to me. Therefore go and make disciples of all nations, baptizing them in the name of the Father and of the Son and of the Holy Spirit, and teaching them to obey everything I have commanded you. And surely I am with you always, to the very end of the age."*

Pretty clear, huh?

What's strange to me is that most Christians I know are not being intentional about leading people to Christ and making disciples by teaching people to obey everything that Jesus taught. Yet this is His command to us. This is not some extra to be added onto Christianity, discipleship is a vital part.

As Jesus' followers, discipling others is not optional.

Now you may not feel like you have anything to offer or that you are qualified to disciple others. But because of Jesus in you, you have all you need and God can use anyone who is willing and available, yup, even you. This doesn't mean that you will be perfect, the Bible is clear that Jesus is the only one who is perfect. But you can still lead others toward Jesus, even with your imperfections.

So for starters, begin to think about your friends and how you might help them get closer to Jesus. **I challenge you to pray today about who God wants you to disciple.**

This might be another Christian you know, maybe someone at youth group or a friend at school. This could even be a person who is not a believer yet. And I would suggest every Christian should have at least one believer they are discipling and one non-believer that they are actively trying to lead to Jesus. And it doesn't matter where people are at in their spiritual journey, you can meet them where they're at and take them where you're going— towards becoming more like Jesus.

But here's the deal, this making disciples thing will take love and commitment. Jesus spent a lot of time with His disciples. I mean, like I mentioned earlier, He was basically on a three year camping trip with these dudes. And He called them His friends (John 15:15) because they were more than just a project for Him to fix. He cared about them. Jesus was close with the people He discipled and you should be too.

The main way to grow close to people is through spending time together. This doesn't mean that you have to start a whole new set of activities, coming up with "discipleship games" or something like that. Just do life and invite the people you are pouring into to come along with you.

What hobbies do you have? What things do you enjoy doing? Even what responsibilities do you need to take care of? These can all be ways of spending time with those you are mentoring.

For instance, if you love soccer, invite others to go kick the ball around. And then during your time of hanging out, bring God up. Share something that you are currently learning or even something that you are struggling with. Remember, you don't always have to have it all together to disciple others. And you don't need to force talking about Jesus the whole time. Go with the conversation, be their friend, ask how they're doing and even just get to know what they like and don't like.

With your Christian friends, you want to challenge them to grow deeper in their personal relationship with God AND to seek out and mentor others too. Walk them through what it means to "recklessly abandon" their lives for Jesus and then inspire them to start making disciples too.

Stick with these friends for the long haul. If they start rocking it and they have their own group of friends they are discipling, then keep encouraging them along the way. Build them up; let them know how good they are doing. Hebrews 3:13 says, *"Encourage one another daily, as long as it is called Today, so that none of you may be hardened by sin's deceitfulness."* We all need encouragement.

If they start struggling, don't give up on them. Continue to pour your time and energy into their lives. They need you. But even more than them needing you, they need Jesus and you just might be the person who continues to remind them of God's love, grace and forgiveness.

Sometimes you might need to call your Christian friends out. You may need to point out an area of sin in their life. You want to be careful when you do this, because you don't want to come off as arrogant, prideful or as if you have it all together. As many have said, a Christian is just one beggar showing other beggars where to find bread. You, yourself, are still in need of bread; you still need Jesus' forgiveness just as much as everyone else. Never forget that.

When Jesus said, *"First take the plank out of your own eye, and then you will see clearly to remove the speck from your brother's eye"* (Matthew 7:3-5), He was laying out how to confront sin. He was not saying, because you yourself are sinful, you can never point out sin in another's life. He was saying when you see the sin in another Christian's life, first look at your own life and realize your own sin. You might see a little something in someone's eye, but check out the mirror to see whether you've got a 2x4 sticking out of yours. As you recognize your areas of sin and go to your friends with that mentality, you will go in humility.

Notice how the verse says *"brother."* This is how you deal with Christians. With non-Christians, it's different; you don't hold them to the same standard. Your goal with them is to point them towards Jesus. So focus on talking about how great Jesus is, how everyone needs Him, what He did for us and how they can find freedom in Him.

Those you're discipling should want to spend time with you. So your goal is not to be the person who tells them all that they're doing wrong. Nor should you just sit around quoting Bible verses to them. Have fun, do life and point people to Jesus along the way.

Remember, Jesus was a fun guy to be around. You see Him getting invited to parties and I feel like the only people you invite to a party are the people who know how to have a good time. He wanted to move people past the Pharisee's lists of do's and don'ts and point them toward a life filled with joy, laughter, excitement, meaning and adventure.

Another thing to remember is that making disciples doesn't mean that you try to get others to worship and follow Jesus in the exact same way you do. **You should be all about pointing them to the ultimate disciple maker—Jesus, so that they can respond to how He is forming each person uniquely.**

God is going to express different parts of His character through our particular uniqueness, in order to give the world a fuller picture of who He is. This is part of what it looks like to be the Church, Jesus Christ's body on earth made up of many parts, all submitted to the head, Jesus Himself (1 Corinthians 12).

It's like He is conducting a magnificent orchestra that requires each of us to play our own part so that He can direct the entire ensemble to play beautiful music together.

These parts can look very different. For example, sometimes the part God calls people to play is fun and exciting, but sometimes it's really, really difficult. And it is beyond our ability to understand the ways of God and why some people's journey includes incredible suffering for Him and others' seem pretty pain free.

But that's why it's so important that each person ultimately take their cues from God first and foremost. We can help each other in this process. But in the end, He is the one and only one who must be the focus of this quest to live the life God has called us to.

So here's the question. **Will you join me in sharing Jesus' message and mentoring others?**

I believe this generation of Christians is like a sleeping giant. I encounter students all across the nation who believe in Jesus, but are struggling to find the boldness to love and live like Him in their schools and neighborhoods. What if every teenage Christian were to awake to the mission at hand, arise from the slumber of selfishness, embracing His characteristics as their own and love and live with reckless abandonment for Jesus and His cause—THE Cause?

FOLLOW ME...

AS I FOLLOW JESUS

[When my pastor, Doug Horch, designed this t-shirt he reminded me, "This is what every Christian should be able to say. 'Follow me.'"]

What if you and all your Christian friends started making disciples who make disciples?

You would be an unstoppable force of world change.

And to finish the Zane t-shirt story, the shirt got made, but we added to the caption so it read: "Follow me...as I follow Jesus." It was still awkward. And still is. But it has challenged me in ways that I am thankful for, calling me to a new standard, reminding me of the words of Paul in Ephesians 4:1, *"Live a life worthy of the calling you have received."*

Maybe no one has made a shirt with you on it looking all goofy with the caption, "Follow me… as I follow Jesus." But every single one of us should strive to be able to wear just such a shirt with confidence as we follow Him. Let's strive to say like Paul in 1 Corinthians 11:1, *"Follow my example, as I follow the example of Christ."*

12
I'M ALL IN

Now GO!

I will never forget the first guy who really discipled me. His name is Bryan Bartels. Within the first week of meeting him he was like, "Hey, you want to go street witnessing?" I didn't even know what that meant. But he sounded excited, so I went. At this point in time I had only been a Christian for about a month or so. I was in for a surprise.

As we were driving toward the nearest city, I started getting nervous, because Bryan was getting more and more excited. He was talking about witnessing, street preaching, evangelizing and all sorts of other things that I had no clue about. I remember at one point he started talking about how the most important thing, no matter what else we do, was that we gotta give them the gospel. I know this might sound weird, but I didn't even know what the "gospel" was. I mean, I knew the message about Jesus, but I was so new to all this Christianese (Christians' foreign language), that I didn't know what he meant by the "gospel."

I was really freaking out. I realized I was in way over my head. There were two other dudes with us and they were all stoked. I was the only one without a clue to what was happening.

Midway through my thoughts about how I could either jump from the car, hide out in a bathroom when we got there or fake like I all of a sudden lost my voice, I heard Bryan start talking about these things called tracts. Which was more Christianese. But as he explained these little cards that we could hand out he said, "The best thing is they have the gospel right on them."

It was like I heard those words in slow motion and then they echoed through my head. Secretly, I slipped one from the pile and began to read it discreetly, as though I was trying to find some top secret information. Of course, I found out that the gospel is the story about Jesus, His life, death, resurrection and what it means for us.

Without meaning to, I exclaimed out loud, "So dumb…the gospel!" What I meant was that it was dumb that I didn't know the secret code words, but that wasn't how it came out.

Everybody was like, "Uh, what?"

That was the first of many trips, excursions, outings and experiences.

Bryan didn't just talk with me about what it looked like to follow Jesus, he showed me. I don't even think Bryan had a thought-out plan for how to "disciple" people. He was just crazy about loving and living for Jesus and he just invited people to join him in doing the same.

I remember when he taught me about prayer. He snuck into my room at like 6 a.m., got right next to my face and said, "HEY!" He about gave me a heart attack, wondering why this strange person had practically crawled into my bed and was now inches from my face, staring at me with crazy eyes.

Then he said, "Are you awake?"

"Of course, I am awake...NOW!"

"Okay, sweet, then let's go pray," he said, still looking at me with crazy eyes. So we went and prayed. He didn't have to preach a sermon to me about the importance of prayer or how to pray, he just showed me. Rather than just talk about prayer, we prayed. Now sure, there were times when he would talk about the importance of prayer and he would talk with me about how to pray, but mostly, he just showed me.

Bryan didn't come up with some "12 steps to effective discipleship" and then get a booklet for me to work through. He was pursuing God and living for God and he simply invited me along with him.

You may not feel like you have the right resources, or the full outline of what discipleship looks like, but at some time we just have to GO! Like Nike says, "Just Do It."

Just Do It

If you want some resources to help with studying the Bible or a set of devotions to walk your friends through, check out dare2share.org. You can find lots of free devos there or you can pick up an inexpensive downloadable guide called "Now Grow" from their store. It includes seven interactive Bible studies that will help answer seven main questions for a new believer and is actually really helpful for any believer—new or old.

When Jesus said *"go and make disciples"* (Matthew 28:19), the word "go" in the context of this verse could also be translated "as you go." "As you go" about your daily life, go with a new purpose.

"As you go" to soccer practice make it about more than just running drills and practicing soccer, make friends with someone new for the sake of telling them about Jesus. "As you go" to school look for the loner and sit next to them at lunch and ask them about their life and beliefs. "As you go" to the movies with your friends share with them about the points in the movie that relate to God or sin. "As you go" to the mall invite a Christian friend with you and make it a goal for each of you to start a spiritual conversation with one person before you leave. "As you go" to your friend's house to hang out look for opportunities in regular conversation to bring God up.

Rather than waiting for the next missions trip to "go," look at everyday, regular activities as an opportunity to disciple others "as you go."

This may still mean that you have to "go" places you have never gone or try things you have never done. For instance, God may send you to "go" overseas and be a missionary or He may send you to "go" on a week-long trip with your church. He may send you to "go" to the inner city to reach out to the homeless or He may send you to "go" only heaven knows where and you'll need to "go."

Or say you only have Christian friends. If that's the case, you will need to start something new in order to build relationships with people who don't know Jesus. That would be a great opportunity to get some of your Christian friends together and try one of these ideas:

- Join a sports team together or go to the local gym together and start new relationships
- Start a new hobby together where you meet new people
- Go to the local park and toss the frisbee around and invite other teenagers to join you
- Get creative and think of ways you can invest in the lives of your Christian friends and meet new friends.

The point is you may need to "go" to something entirely new and you may need to "go" to the same old places with a new purpose and focus. Either way, "going" should be something you do every day "as you go" about regular life.

I'll never forget the first time I really saw this "as you go" approach to following Jesus actually lived out by a teenager.

RECKLESS

I first met this student named Shane when he and his youth group came to the Torchbearers Center on a summer retreat. We took the students mountain biking, hiking, climbing and out for all sorts of other Rocky Mountain adventures. It was awesome. But even more awesome was the conversation I had with Shane one day sitting around the dinner table.

We were talking about what it really looks like to follow Jesus. We started talking about living recklessly for God, making disciples and reaching out to non-believers with the gospel.

I will never forget the look on Shane's face when he slammed the table with his hands, stood up and said with authority, "I'm all in."

Before Shane left I gave him my email address so we could keep up as he went home and faced the reality of living it all out. Two days after they'd left I got a message from Shane saying that on his way home with his youth group they'd stopped at a gas station and some lady had asked him about the headband he was wearing. It was his youth group logo, so Shane instantly thought *this is one of those opportunities that Zane was talking about*. So Shane shared the gospel. At the end of the email he was fired up.

Then he decided to gather up some of his Christian friends from youth group and together they agreed to pray around the flagpole every day before school. So they did. But the whole first week it rained practically every day!

Shane got super discouraged, but decided that he was not going to let that stop him. The next week they were out there again, but this time no rain. As they were praying around the flagpole another student came up and was like, "What are you guys doing out here? You looked crazy standing out here in the rain every day."

Shane said, "Oh, we've just been praying that God would use us to reach our school with the gospel and that students would come to know God and make Him known."

The kid said, "Oh, that sounds pretty cool. What if a person wanted to know more about God?"

Shane got a little excited so he answered, "We have a Bible study where people can come learn about God." Shane's friends looked at him like, "We do?" Shane whispered back, "We do now!"

So then Shane emailed me freaking out, "What do I do?!" I told him about these podcasts that Dare

2 Share has online and that he could download them and just play them.

So Shane went home and said, "Hey Mom, some friends are going to be coming over." His mom gave him the look that every teenager knows and it's not good. But Shane continued, "They're coming for a Bible study."

Now mom was stoked. "I'll put out some snacks and bake some cookies."

During the podcasts, Greg Stier from Dare 2 Share always gives an opportunity for people to become believers and kids started getting saved! Now Shane was fully freaking out. But Shane and his crew got creative in looking for all sorts of different ways to reach out at school.

Shane started seeing his football team as a perfect opportunity. He started sitting next to different kids after each game on the bus. One day he sat next to a guy that knew Shane was a Christian, but now Shane was a Christian on a mission. Shane got into a conversation, then brought up Jesus and they dove into an intense discussion where the kid shared about how his mom had died when he was 12 and before that his dad abused him. If God is so loving, then how could God let that happen?

Shane thought of one of the Dare 2 Share podcasts where Greg talked about never meeting his own dad and how angry he was at his dad, until one day he realized that while he may not know his father on earth, he had a perfect daddy in heaven. The kid began to weep and Shane laid out the gospel for him and he accepted Christ right there on the football bus.

Shane then wrote me, "I'm witnessing people who used to be my friends back when I wasn't living the right way come to know Christ. It's blowing my mind. I've seen the infinite power of God and the power of prayer."

Do you want to experience the infinite power of God and the power of prayer in your life?

Then like Shane, you need to realize that living and giving God's love can happen every day "as you go." You'll be making disciples all along the way.

That's what Bryan did with me. **He met me where I was at and took me where he was going—to Jesus.** I will never forget it, because it changed my life forever. He met me where I was at in my journey with Jesus, helped me to stay on the path and encouraged me all along the way so I didn't

grow tired or weary. I am forever indebted to Bryan
for the investment he made in my life.

But Bryan wasn't doing anything new that hadn't
been done before. He was just "following Jesus" in
the truest sense. He knew that following Him wasn't
just a personal thing to be done in private. True,
passionate followers of Jesus help others to follow,
as well. **They make disciples who make disciples,
who make disciples, who make disciples, until
the whole world is following Jesus.**

And this is where we move from addition in trying
to reach the world to multiplication.

Rather than you personally trying to tell every
person in the world about Jesus—adding one
person by one person to God's kingdom—your
goal is to train others to help you multiply the
process out.

To illustrate this point, here's how it would play out
in just thirty days if just one person got serious
about making disciples who make disciples.

Day one starts with one lone believer. Then on
day two, say they led one person to Christ and
taught them how to share their faith, as well, so
now there'd be two disciples. Then on day three,

[The Power of Multiplication]

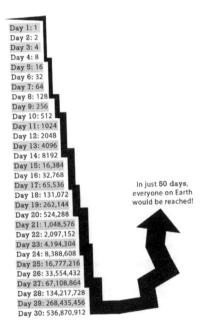

Day 1: 1
Day 2: 2
Day 3: 4
Day 4: 8
Day 5: 16
Day 6: 32
Day 7: 64
Day 8: 128
Day 9: 256
Day 10: 512
Day 11: 1024
Day 12: 2048
Day 13: 4096
Day 14: 8192
Day 15: 16,384
Day 16: 32,768
Day 17: 65,536
Day 18: 131,072
Day 19: 262,144
Day 20: 524,288
Day 21: 1,048,576
Day 22: 2,097,152
Day 23: 4,194,304
Day 24: 8,388,608
Day 25: 16,777,216
Day 26: 33,554,432
Day 27: 67,108,864
Day 28: 134,217,728
Day 29: 268,435,456
Day 30: 536,870,912

In just 50 days, everyone on Earth would be reached!

say each of them led someone else to Christ, so there'd be four disciples.

And on day four, again each of these four led another person to Christ, so there'd be eight disciples. Day five, you're up to 16 disciples. Day six, 32 followers. By day seven, just one week into this process, there'd be 64…and on and on the disciple-cycles would go from there.

I know it doesn't seem to be multiplying by crazy amounts just yet, but watch what happens as the days progress in the chart.

You soon see the astounding results. By day 30, there'd be 536,870,912 followers of Jesus who were serious about sharing their faith and following Him.

The crazy thing is, at the end of just 50 days, it would be possible to reach every person on this earth![2]

Maybe this is why Paul tells Timothy (his disciple) in 2 Timothy 2:2, *"The things you have heard me say in the presence of many witnesses entrust to reliable men who will also be qualified to teach others."* Paul knew the impact of multiplying discipleship, so he nurtured and challenged his disciple, Timothy, to in turn disciple others.

This was Jesus' model in spreading the gospel. Most of His time during His ministry on earth was spent with 12 disciples. Sure, He had times where He spoke to the masses, like when He fed the 5,000, but most of His time was spent pouring His life into just 12 followers. He was teaching them, mentoring them, showing them how to love God and love others. And eventually, these 12 guys turned the world upside down, making an impact still felt today, 2,000 years later!

Do you want to witness God at work in others' lives and experience Him at work in your own life? Make disciples! Begin pouring out God's love to those around you. Follow Jesus by reaching out to those in need. Invite others along with you. Show those

[I'm all in! Are you?]

153

around you what it means to be a follower of Jesus by loving and living for God with all your heart, soul, mind and strength and invite them to do the same.

It's time for you to recklessly abandon all and follow Him to the point of no return!

The adventure of following Jesus is going to involve great cost, but I promise it will bring even greater payoff. The first followers of Jesus actually left everything. They left their nets, families, friends and prior plans about what their future might look like. In one sense, they lost it all. But I bet if you could ask them, they would say what they gained was far greater. They lived full lives of incredible adventure as they made disciples who made disciples. They followed Jesus to the point of no return and they changed the course of history!

This is the model of Jesus.

And if Jesus Himself made disciples, recklessly abandoning His life to do His Father's will, then so should we.

So be reckless. Risk it all. Give it all. Because there is no greater joy than living fully for Jesus.

John 14:21 sums it up for us, *"Whoever has my commands and keeps them is the one who loves me. The one who loves me will be loved by my Father, and I too will love them and show myself to them"* (NIV, 2011).

Jesus is calling you to abandon all, follow Him and make disciples. Now GO!

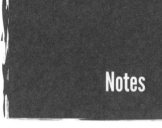

Notes

[1]Josh McDowell, *The New Evidence that Demands a Verdict* (Nashville: Thomas Nelson, 1999), page 193.

[2]Raivyn's Roost, *What if a Penny was Doubled Every Day for a Year,* http://raivynnsroost.blogspot.com/2007/02/what-if-penny-was-doubled-every-day-for.html.

About the Author

After years of living for cheap thrills and temporary highs, Zane Black experienced a radical encounter with Jesus that changed his life forever. Zane's lifestyle of drugs and alcohol became a thing of the past as he found a new adventure in an "all out" life with Jesus. Zane loves sharing about the love and power of God that rocked his world, in hopes that students will encounter Jesus and live "all out" lives for Him as well. Zane has had the opportunity to share at Torchbearer Bible Schools, Dare 2 Share conferences, Creation Fest and at local churches. He took part in both *GOSPEL Journey* reality series and is the author of two previous books, *InZane* and *Shreddin the Gnar* and the faith sharing tool *Get Stoked*.

A Final Note from the Author

If you made it this far and aren't totally annoyed and fed up with me, if you actually want to hear from me more, you can connect with me via:

Facebook: Zane Black
Twitter: @zaneblack
www.zaneblack.com

INZANE

by Zane Black

Zane's life story will inspire you to live for Christ! Told in his raw, honest, conversational style, *InZane...Totally Stoked on this Jesus Dude* captures Zane's journey from a party boy to a committed Christian. His story will keep you turning the page, and at the same time challenge you to put Jesus at the center of your life.

GET STOKED

by Zane Black

Use Zane's story to get your friends thinking about Jesus! In this creative, engaging pocketsize booklet, Zane briefly shares his story and provides a clear explanation of the gospel and its power to change lives. Pick up some copies of *Get Stoked* today and give one to each of your friends who need Jesus.

VENTI JESUS PLEASE

by Greg Stier

A perfect tool to reach your unbelieving friends. For anyone who's ever wondered about spiritual things, listening in on this conversation between three high school friends could open up a whole new world of possibilities. A perfect tool to reach an unbelieving teenager.

These and other great resources available at **www.dare2share.org**

DARE 2 SHARE ON YOUR PHONE

This mobile app will help train and inspire you to share your faith with your friends wherever you go! Go to **dare2share.org/mobileapp** to download the FREE Dare 2 Share app.

DARE 2 SHARE IN YOUR INBOX

Sign up for Soul Fuel from Dare 2 Share and get weekly emails that use music, movies, TV and trends to inspire you to live for THE Cause of Christ! View the most current article and sign up to receive Soul Fuel weekly at **dare2share.org/students**

DARE 2 SHARE CONFERENCES

Join us at Dare 2 Share's weekend student evangelism training conferences, as well as youth leader training events. Current events schedule available at **dare2share.org/conferences**